THIS BOOK BELONGS TO
The Library of

....

....

I can't tell you how grateful I am that you decided to read my book. My most heartfelt thanks that you took time out of your life to choose my work and I hope you find benefit within these pages.

There are so many books available today that offer similar content so that makes it even more humbling that you decided to buying mine.

Tell me what you thought! I am eager to hear your opinion and ideas on what you read as are others who are looking for a good book to buy.

Leave a review on Amazon.com so others can benefit from your wisdom!

With much thanks.

Table of Contents

Crochet Mastery Discover Over 80 Modern Crochet Projects in this Comprehensive Book

SUMMARY

The book provides a comprehensive overview of the subject matter, covering various aspects and providing a holistic understanding of the topic. It delves into the historical background, exploring the origins and development of the subject, and traces its evolution over time. The author presents a well-researched and well-structured narrative, offering a balanced perspective and incorporating different viewpoints.

The book also examines the key themes and concepts related to the subject, providing in-depth analysis and critical insights. It explores the underlying theories and frameworks, discussing their relevance and applicability in different contexts. The author presents a range of case studies and examples, illustrating the practical implications and real-world applications of the subject matter.

Furthermore, the book engages with the current debates and controversies surrounding the topic, presenting different arguments and counterarguments. It encourages readers to think critically and form their own opinions, while also providing a comprehensive overview of the existing literature and research on the subject. The author highlights the gaps in knowledge and suggests avenues for further exploration and research.

In addition, the book incorporates a multidisciplinary approach, drawing on insights from various fields such as psychology, sociology, economics, and political science. It explores the intersections and interconnections between different disciplines, offering a holistic understanding of the subject matter. The author also incorporates diverse perspectives and voices, ensuring a comprehensive and inclusive analysis.

Overall, the book provides a thorough and detailed overview of the subject, catering to both beginners and experts in the field. It is a valuable resource for students, researchers, and professionals seeking to deepen their understanding and knowledge of the topic. The author's engaging writing style and comprehensive approach make it an enjoyable and informative read.

The art of crochet, a traditional craft that involves creating fabric by interlocking loops of yarn with a hooked needle, has experienced a remarkable resurgence in recent years. Once considered a pastime of grandmothers and a dying art form, crochet has now become a popular and trendy hobby embraced by people of all ages and backgrounds.

One of the reasons for the resurgence of crochet is its versatility and the endless possibilities it offers for creativity. Crochet allows individuals to create a wide range of items, from clothing and accessories to home decor and even intricate works of art. With just a few basic stitches, one can create beautiful and intricate patterns, making crochet a highly rewarding and satisfying craft.

Furthermore, the accessibility of crochet has contributed to its resurgence. Unlike other crafts that require expensive equipment or specialized skills, crochet can be learned with just a few basic supplies and a willingness to learn. There are countless online tutorials, books, and classes available that make it easy for beginners to get started and progress at their own pace. This accessibility has attracted a new generation of crafters who are eager to explore their creativity and express themselves through crochet.

In addition, the resurgence of crochet can be attributed to the growing interest in sustainable and eco-friendly practices. As people become more conscious of the environmental impact of fast fashion and mass-produced goods, they are turning to crafts like crochet as a way to create their own unique and sustainable items. Crocheting allows individuals to repurpose yarn and materials, reducing waste and promoting a more sustainable lifestyle.

The resurgence of crochet has also been fueled by the sense of community and connection it fosters. Crochet groups and online communities have sprung up, providing a space for crafters to share their work, seek advice, and connect with like-minded individuals. This sense of community has not only encouraged more people to take up crochet but has also created a supportive and inclusive environment where crafters can learn from each other and inspire one another.

Furthermore, the therapeutic benefits of crochet have also contributed to its resurgence. Many people find crochet to be a calming and meditative activity that helps reduce stress and anxiety. The repetitive motions and focus required in crochet can provide a sense of mindfulness and relaxation, making it a popular form of self-care and a way to unwind from the demands of daily life.

A. Tools and materials

When it comes to completing any task or project, having the right tools and materials is essential. Whether you are a professional or a DIY enthusiast, having a well-stocked toolbox can make all the difference in the outcome of your project.

First and foremost, having a variety of hand tools is crucial. This includes items such as screwdrivers, wrenches, pliers, hammers, and tape measures. These tools are versatile and can be used for a wide range of tasks, from assembling furniture to fixing a leaky faucet. It is important to have different sizes and types of each tool to accommodate various projects.

Power tools are another essential component of any toolbox. These tools are designed to make tasks easier and more efficient. Some common power tools include drills, saws, sanders, and routers. Depending on the nature of your projects, you may also need specialized power tools such as a tile cutter or a nail gun. It is important to invest in high-quality power tools that are durable and reliable.

In addition to hand and power tools, having the right materials is equally important. This includes items such as screws, nails, bolts, and adhesives. It is important to have a variety of sizes and types of fasteners to accommodate different materials and applications. Additionally, having a selection of different adhesives, such as wood glue, epoxy, and super glue, can be useful for bonding various materials together.

When it comes to construction or renovation projects, having the right building materials is crucial. This includes items such as lumber, drywall, insulation, and flooring materials. It is important to choose materials that are appropriate for the specific project and meet the necessary safety and building code requirements. Additionally, having the right tools to work with these materials, such as a circular saw or a drywall knife, is essential for achieving professional results.

Safety equipment is another important aspect of any toolbox. This includes items such as safety glasses, gloves, ear protection, and dust masks. It is crucial to prioritize safety when working with tools and materials, as accidents can happen. Wearing the appropriate safety equipment can help prevent injuries and ensure a safe working environment.

Lastly, having a well-organized toolbox is essential for efficiency and productivity. Investing in a toolbox or tool chest with compartments and dividers can help keep your tools and materials organized and easily accessible. This will save you time and frustration when searching for a specific tool or material.

Understanding crochet patterns is an essential skill for anyone interested in the art of crochet. Crochet patterns serve as a guide for creating various stitches, shapes, and designs using a crochet hook and yarn. They provide step-by-step instructions on how to create specific stitches, how many stitches to make, and where to make them in order to achieve the desired outcome.

To fully understand crochet patterns, it is important to familiarize oneself with the different symbols, abbreviations, and terms commonly used in crochet patterns. These symbols and abbreviations represent different stitches and techniques, and understanding them is crucial for following the instructions accurately. Common symbols include ch for chain stitch, sc for single crochet, dc for double crochet, and so on. By learning these symbols and abbreviations, crocheters can easily decipher the instructions and execute the stitches correctly.

Another important aspect of understanding crochet patterns is grasping the concept of gauge. Gauge refers to the number of stitches and rows per inch achieved when crocheting with a specific hook size and yarn. It is crucial to match the gauge mentioned in the pattern to ensure that the finished project turns out the correct size and shape. Crocheters can achieve the correct gauge by using the recommended hook size and yarn mentioned in the pattern, or by adjusting their tension while crocheting.

Furthermore, understanding the structure of crochet patterns is essential. Crochet patterns typically consist of multiple sections, including a materials list, stitch abbreviations, and the actual pattern instructions. The materials list outlines the specific yarn, hook size, and any additional materials required for the project. The stitch abbreviations section provides a reference for the symbols and abbreviations used in the pattern. Finally, the pattern instructions guide crocheters through the step-by-step process of creating the desired project.

In addition to these technical aspects, understanding crochet patterns also involves developing a sense of creativity and intuition. While patterns provide a foundation, they can also be modified and customized to suit individual preferences. Crocheters can experiment with different yarn colors, stitch combinations, and embellishments to add their personal touch to the project. This creative aspect of crochet patterns allows for endless possibilities and encourages crocheters to explore their own unique style.

In conclusion, understanding crochet patterns is crucial for successfully creating beautiful crochet projects. By familiarizing oneself with the symbols, abbreviations, and terms commonly used in crochet patterns, crocheters can easily follow the instructions and execute the stitches accurately.

Increasing and decreasing stitches are two fundamental techniques used in knitting and crochet to shape the fabric and create various patterns and designs. These techniques are essential for creating garments, accessories, and other knitted or crocheted items with a desired fit and shape.

Increasing stitches involve adding new stitches to the fabric, which results in the fabric becoming wider or larger. There are several methods for increasing stitches, including yarn overs, make one (M1), knit front and back (KFB), and others. Yarn overs are commonly used in lace knitting to create decorative holes or eyelets. Make one (M1) is a method where a new stitch is created by picking up the horizontal strand between two stitches and knitting or purling into it. Knit front and back (KFB) involves knitting into the front and back loops of the same stitch, effectively creating two stitches from one.

On the other hand, decreasing stitches involve removing stitches from the fabric, resulting in a narrower or smaller fabric. Decreasing stitches are commonly used to shape the fabric, create curves, or form specific patterns. Some common methods for decreasing stitches include knit two together (K2tog), slip slip knit (SSK), and purl two together (P2tog). Knit two together (K2tog) is a method where two stitches are knit together as one, effectively decreasing the stitch count by one. Slip slip knit (SSK) involves slipping two stitches individually as if to knit, then knitting them together through the back loops. Purl two together (P2tog) is similar to K2tog, but it is used when working in purl stitches.

Both increasing and decreasing stitches require careful attention to maintain an even tension and ensure that the fabric remains balanced. It is important to follow the pattern instructions or charts accurately to achieve the desired shape and design. These techniques can be used in combination to create intricate patterns, such as cables, lace, or shaping for garments like sweaters, hats, and socks.

In summary, increasing and decreasing stitches are essential techniques in knitting and crochet that allow for shaping and creating various patterns and designs. By adding or removing stitches, the fabric can be shaped to fit the desired form and achieve the desired aesthetic. These techniques require practice and attention to detail, but they open up a world of possibilities for creating beautiful and unique knitted or crocheted items.

Working in the round refers to a technique used in knitting or crochet where the project is worked continuously in a circular motion, rather than in rows or back and forth. This technique is commonly used for creating seamless items such as hats, socks, and sleeves.

To work in the round, you will need circular knitting needles or double-pointed needles, depending on the size of your project. Circular needles have two needle tips connected by a flexible cable, while double-pointed needles come in sets of four or five.

To begin working in the round, you will cast on the required number of stitches onto your needles. Make sure the stitches are evenly distributed around the needles if using circular needles or divided evenly among the double-pointed needles.

Once your stitches are cast on, you will join the round by bringing the first stitch of the round to meet the last stitch, being careful not to twist the stitches. This creates a continuous loop of stitches.

When working in the round, you will typically use the knit stitch for every round, unless you are incorporating other stitch patterns or techniques. To knit in the round, simply insert your right needle into the first stitch on your left needle, wrap the yarn around the right needle, and pull it through the stitch, sliding the old stitch off the left needle. Repeat this process for each stitch until you have completed the round.

If you are working on a project with a large number of stitches, such as a sweater, you may find it easier to use circular needles. The flexible cable allows you to comfortably hold a large number of stitches without them falling off the needles.

Working in the round can be a bit tricky at first, especially when joining the round and avoiding twists in your stitches. However, with practice and patience, you will become more comfortable with this technique and be able to create beautiful seamless projects.

The output of the input A. Gauge and tension refers to the measurement and level of tightness or pressure applied to a particular object or system. Gauge typically refers to the measurement of a physical quantity, such as the thickness or diameter of a wire, the pressure of a fluid, or the size of a needle. Tension, on the other hand, refers to the force or stress applied to an object or system, often resulting in the stretching or elongation of materials.

When considering gauge and tension together, it usually implies the relationship between the measurement and the level of force or pressure being applied. For example, in the context of a wire, the gauge would indicate its thickness, while the tension would represent the amount of force or stress being exerted on the wire. Similarly, in the case of a fluid, the gauge would measure the pressure, while the tension would reflect the level of force being applied to the fluid.

The output of the input A. Gauge and tension could vary depending on the specific context or application. It could involve providing numerical values or measurements for the gauge and tension, indicating the appropriate range or level for optimal performance or safety. Additionally, the output might involve analyzing the relationship between gauge and tension, identifying any potential issues or concerns, and suggesting adjustments or modifications to ensure the desired outcome.

In summary, the output of the input A. Gauge and tension encompasses the measurement and level of tightness or pressure applied to an object or system, considering factors such as gauge, which measures a physical quantity, and tension, which represents the force or stress being exerted. The output could involve providing numerical values, analyzing the relationship between gauge and tension, and suggesting adjustments or modifications for optimal performance or safety.

Home decor projects can be a fun and creative way to personalize your living space and make it feel more like home. Whether you're looking to update a room, add a pop of color, or simply refresh your decor, there are countless projects you can undertake to achieve the desired look.

One popular home decor project is painting. This can involve anything from painting an accent wall to repainting furniture or even creating a mural. Painting is a relatively inexpensive way to transform a space and can be easily customized to match your personal style. You can choose bold and vibrant colors to make a statement or opt for more muted tones for a calming and serene atmosphere.

Another home decor project that can have a big impact is adding new lighting fixtures. Lighting plays a crucial role in setting the mood and ambiance of a room. By replacing outdated or generic light fixtures with more stylish and unique options, you can instantly elevate the overall look and feel of your space. Consider installing pendant lights over a kitchen island, adding a chandelier in the dining room, or incorporating wall sconces for a touch of elegance.

If you're looking to add texture and warmth to a room, consider incorporating textiles into your decor. This can include anything from throw pillows and blankets to curtains and rugs. Textiles not only add visual interest but also provide comfort and coziness. Choose fabrics that complement your existing color scheme and patterns that add depth and dimension to the space.

For those who enjoy DIY projects, there are endless possibilities when it comes to home decor. You can create your own artwork by painting or drawing, or even try your hand at macrame or weaving. DIY projects allow you to showcase your creativity and add a personal touch to your home. Plus, they can be a great way to save money and repurpose materials you already have.

In conclusion, home decor projects offer a wide range of opportunities to transform your living space and make it uniquely yours. Whether you're a seasoned DIY enthusiast or just starting out, there are projects for every skill level and budget. From painting and lighting to textiles and DIY crafts, the possibilities are endless. So go ahead and unleash your creativity to create a home that reflects your personal style and brings you joy.

A. Garments refer to clothing items that are worn by individuals to cover and protect their bodies. These garments can vary in terms of style, design, material, and purpose. They serve not only as a means of protection but also as a form of self-expression and cultural representation.

Garments can be categorized into various types based on their intended use and the body parts they cover. Some common types of garments include shirts, pants, dresses, skirts, jackets, coats, underwear, and accessories such as hats, scarves, and gloves. Each type of garment serves a specific purpose and is designed to cater to different occasions, climates, and personal preferences.

The design and style of garments can vary greatly depending on factors such as cultural traditions, fashion trends, and individual preferences. Different regions and communities have their own unique clothing styles and traditional garments that reflect their cultural heritage. Fashion trends also play a significant role in shaping the design and aesthetics of garments, with new styles and designs constantly emerging and evolving.

The choice of material used in garments is another important aspect that determines their functionality and comfort. Common materials used in garment production include cotton, silk, wool, linen, polyester, and various synthetic blends. Each material has its own unique properties, such as breathability, durability, and texture, which influence the overall quality and feel of the garment.

Garments not only serve practical purposes but also play a significant role in self-expression and identity. People often choose garments that align with their personal style, preferences, and cultural background. Clothing can be used to convey social status, profession, or even political beliefs. It is a powerful tool for individuals to express their creativity, personality, and individuality.

In addition to individual expression, garments also have a significant impact on the environment and society. The fashion industry is known for its environmental footprint, with issues such as water pollution, waste generation, and carbon emissions associated with garment production. Sustainable and ethical fashion practices are gaining momentum, with a focus on reducing the negative impact of garments on the environment and promoting fair labor practices.

In conclusion, garments are essential items of clothing that serve both practical and expressive purposes. They come in various types, designs, and materials, reflecting cultural traditions, fashion trends, and individual preferences. Garments not only protect and cover the body but also serve as a means of self-expression, identity, and cultural representation.

Complex patterns and techniques refer to intricate and sophisticated designs or methods that require a high level of skill and expertise to understand and execute. These patterns and techniques can be found in various fields such as art, music, mathematics, computer programming, and many others.

In art, complex patterns can be seen in the works of artists who employ intricate designs, intricate brushwork, or intricate compositions. These patterns can be found in various art movements such as pointillism, op art, or Islamic art, where artists create intricate geometric patterns using repetitive shapes and lines. These patterns often require a deep understanding of mathematical principles and a meticulous attention to detail.

In music, complex patterns can be observed in compositions that involve intricate melodies, harmonies, or rhythms. These patterns can be found in genres such as classical music, jazz, or progressive rock, where musicians create intricate musical structures that challenge the listener's perception and require advanced technical skills to perform. These patterns often involve complex time signatures, polyrhythms, or intricate chord progressions.

In mathematics, complex patterns can be found in various branches such as fractal geometry, number theory, or chaos theory. Fractal geometry, for example, explores complex patterns that repeat at different scales, creating intricate and self-similar structures. Number theory deals with complex patterns and relationships among numbers, while chaos theory studies complex and unpredictable patterns that emerge from simple mathematical equations.

In computer programming, complex patterns and techniques are often used to solve intricate problems or optimize algorithms. These patterns can be found in areas such as artificial intelligence, data analysis, or cryptography. For example, in artificial intelligence, complex pattern recognition algorithms are used to analyze large datasets and make predictions or decisions based on the patterns identified. In cryptography, complex encryption algorithms are employed to secure sensitive information and protect it from unauthorized access.

Overall, complex patterns and techniques require a high level of skill, knowledge, and expertise to understand and execute. They can be found in various fields and disciplines, and their exploration and application often lead to advancements and innovations in those areas.

Online crochet communities and forums are virtual spaces where individuals who share a passion for crochet can come together to connect, share ideas, seek advice, and showcase their creations. These communities provide a platform for crocheters of all skill levels, from beginners to experts, to engage in discussions, ask questions, and learn from one another.

One of the key benefits of online crochet communities and forums is the opportunity for crocheters to connect with like-minded individuals from all around the world. These platforms bring together a diverse range of people who are united by their love for crochet, creating a sense of community and camaraderie. Members can share their experiences, stories, and challenges, and find support and encouragement from others who understand their passion.

In these communities, crocheters can also find a wealth of knowledge and resources. Members often share tips, tricks, and techniques, helping each other improve their skills and expand their crochet repertoire. Whether it's learning a new stitch pattern, understanding complex patterns, or troubleshooting common crochet problems, these communities offer a wealth of information that can benefit crocheters at any level.

Furthermore, online crochet communities and forums serve as a platform for inspiration and creativity. Members can showcase their finished projects, share patterns they have created, or seek inspiration for their next crochet endeavor. Seeing the beautiful creations of others can spark new ideas and motivate crocheters to try new techniques or experiment with different yarns and colors.

Another advantage of these communities is the opportunity for crocheters to participate in crochet-alongs and challenges. These events involve a group of crocheters working on the same project or following a specific theme, often with a set timeline. Crochet-alongs and challenges not only provide a fun and interactive way to engage with the community but also offer a chance to learn new skills and complete projects together.

Moreover, online crochet communities and forums are a valuable resource for crocheters looking to buy or sell crochet-related items. Members can find recommendations for yarn brands, hooks, and other crochet supplies, as well as discover online stores or local shops that cater to their needs. Additionally, these platforms often have dedicated sections or threads for members to advertise their handmade crochet items, providing a marketplace for crocheters to showcase and sell their creations.

In conclusion, online crochet communities and forums offer a plethora of benefits for crocheters. They provide a supportive and inclusive environment where individuals can connect, learn, and be inspired.

The journey from being a beginner to achieving mastery in the art of crochet is a truly remarkable and fulfilling experience. It is a process that involves dedication, patience, and a genuine passion for the craft. As one embarks on this journey, they are introduced to the basic techniques and gradually progress towards more complex and intricate patterns.

At the beginning of this journey, a beginner crocheter is often overwhelmed by the sheer amount of information and techniques to learn. They start by familiarizing themselves with the different types of crochet hooks, yarns, and basic stitches such as the chain stitch, single crochet, double crochet, and treble crochet. These foundational stitches serve as building blocks for more advanced patterns and designs.

As the beginner gains confidence and proficiency in the basic stitches, they begin to explore various crochet projects. This could include making simple scarves, hats, or blankets. These projects not only allow the crocheter to practice their skills but also provide a sense of accomplishment and pride in their creations.

As the journey progresses, the crocheter starts to experiment with more complex patterns and techniques. They learn about different stitch combinations, colorwork, and shaping techniques. This opens up a whole new world of possibilities and creativity. The crocheter may choose to challenge themselves by attempting intricate lacework, amigurumi (crocheted stuffed toys), or even garments such as sweaters or shawls.

Throughout this journey, the crocheter also discovers the joy of working with different types of yarns. They learn about the various fibers, weights, and textures available, and how they can greatly impact the final outcome of their projects. This knowledge allows them to make informed choices and create pieces that are not only visually appealing but also comfortable and durable.

As the crocheter continues to practice and refine their skills, they may also explore the world of pattern design. This involves creating their own unique patterns and sharing them with the crochet community. It is a testament to their growth and expertise in the craft.

Achieving mastery in crochet is not just about technical proficiency, but also about developing a deep appreciation for the art form. It is about understanding the history and cultural significance of crochet, and how it has evolved over time. It is about connecting with other crocheters, sharing knowledge, and inspiring each other to push the boundaries of creativity.

Creativity is a powerful force that resides within each and every one of us. It is the ability to think outside the box, to imagine new possibilities, and to express ourselves in unique and innovative ways. However, sometimes we may find ourselves feeling stuck or uninspired, unsure of how to tap into our creative potential. This is where encouragement to explore our creativity becomes crucial.

Encouragement to explore our creativity is like a gentle nudge that pushes us out of our comfort zones and into the realm of endless possibilities. It is the motivation we need to take risks, to try new things, and to embrace the unknown. When we are encouraged to explore our creativity, we are given the freedom to experiment, to make mistakes, and to learn from them. This process of trial and error is essential for growth and development as it allows us to discover what works and what doesn't, ultimately leading us to uncover our true creative potential.

Furthermore, encouragement to explore our creativity helps us to break free from the constraints of societal norms and expectations. It empowers us to challenge the status quo, to question the existing systems, and to envision a better future. By encouraging us to explore our creativity, we are reminded that there are no limits to what we can achieve and that our ideas have the power to shape the world around us.

Moreover, encouragement to explore our creativity fosters a sense of self-belief and confidence. When we are supported and encouraged to pursue our creative endeavors, we begin to believe in our own abilities and talents. We start to trust our instincts and intuition, knowing that our unique perspectives and ideas are valuable contributions to the world. This self-belief not only fuels our creative endeavors but also spills over into other aspects of our lives, empowering us to take on new challenges and overcome obstacles with resilience and determination.

In addition, encouragement to explore our creativity opens up a world of opportunities for personal growth and fulfillment. When we allow ourselves to explore our creative passions, we embark on a journey of self-discovery and self-expression. We uncover hidden talents, develop new skills, and gain a deeper understanding of ourselves and the world around us. This process of exploration and growth not only brings us joy and fulfillment but also allows us to connect with others who share our passions and interests, creating a sense of community and belonging.

Summer Crochet
10 Projects Of Sexy Crochet Bikini

Introduction

Crochet bikinis may not sound like anything special to you, but wait to see the patterns in this book. Some are easy and beginner-friendly, some are more suitable for those more experienced crochet lovers, but one is for sure. You'll have so much fun working on these projects.

To make sure that you are on the right track, read a whole pattern first to check whether you are clear with all the steps. One important thing to mention here is that the book uses abbreviations such as the ones below.

Ch = chain

Sc = single crochet

Dc = double crochet

Tr = treble / triple crochet Hdc = half double crochet Sl st = slip stitch

Yo = yarn over

Now that we have got this, we can move on. At the beginning of any project, you will have to determine the size. The instructions given in the book correspond to the smallest size (S). To get bigger sizes, you should just make a bigger chain, work additional rows or increase over more rows than specified in the patterns.

Once you finish your projects, to make sure that the pattern really opens up, you should make use of the so-called blocking. This is an easy step, which can quickly be done following this method. Lay your bikini on a flat surface and cover it with a damp towel or cloth.

Pay attention that the cloth is not wet too much because the point here is to "steam" the bikini. Then, take you iron, set it on low or medium and press over the damp cloth. Make quick movements (don't keep the iron on the cloth for more than 2 seconds). In just a few minutes, your bikini will be ready to show it off.

Have fun crocheting and enjoy this summer with your new bikini!

Chapter 1 – Grace Bikini

BIKINI TOP

ROW 1

Ch 15 and begin the first row with a sc in the second chain from the hook. Continue working scs in every chain across the row. When you come to the last chain, work 5 scs. Use a stitch marker to mark the center sc. Do not turn your work.

Now, you will have to work into the other side of the chain. So, work a sc in each rem loop of the chain across the row. You should end up with 31 scs or more depending on the size you are making. Turn your work.

ROW 2

Ch 1 and work a sc in every sc from the previous row. Turn your work.

ROW 3

Begin with ch 1 and work a sc in each sc till you come to the center sc. Here, work 5 scs and continue with 1 sc until the end of the row. Turn your work.

ROW 4

This row is the same as Row 2.

ROW 5

Ch 1 and work a sc till you come to the center sc. Work 3 scs and continue working a sc in each sc until you come to the end of the row. Turn your work.

HOW TO CONTINUE?

Repeat the last four rows four times (or more depending on the size). Then, repeat Row 2 once, and you should end up with 61 scs.

HOW TO FINISH?

Working from the wrong side, do a sc in each of the first 3 scs. *Ch 1, skip the next sc and work a sc in each of the next 2 scs. Repeat from* until you come to the last sc where you should do a sc and turn your work.

Again, ch 1 and work a sc in the first sc. *Work 5 dcs in the next chain-1 space and then work a sc in the next chain-1 space. Repeat from* until you reach the last 3 scs. Work a sc in each of these scs.

Repeat the same pattern to make another cup.

HOW TO JOIN THE CUPS?

To join the cups, ch 95. With the wrong side of the piece facing, work a sc row across the bottom of the first cup. Ch 4 and work scs across the second cup as well. Ch 96 and turn your work.

Work a sl st in every chain starting from the second chain from the hook. Then, work a sc in the following 28 scs.

Continue by working a sc in each of the next 4 chains and then work a sc in each of the remaining 28 scs. Work a sl st in each of the next 95 chains.

NECK TIES

With the right side of the piece facing, join the yarn to the top center group of 5 dcs using a sl st. Then, ch 106 and work a sl st in each chain starting from the second chain from the hook.

Repeat the same for the second cup.

BOTTOM PART

Begin crocheting the back part by ch 63.

ROW 1

Work a sc in the second chain from the hook. Continue working a sc in each chain until the end of the row. You should end up with 62 scs. Turn your work.

ROW 2

Ch 1 and work a sc in each sc across the row. Turn your work.

BACK PART

ROW 1

With the right side of the work facing, draw up a loop in each of the first 2 stitches. Yarn over and draw through all the loops on your hook. This creates sc2tog. Work a sc in each sc till you come to the last two scs where you will work a sc2tog in each. Turn your work.

ROW 2

Ch 1 and work a sc in each stitch till you come to the end of the row. Turn your work.

Repeat the last two rows until you end up with 14 stitches.

NEXT ROW

With the right side facing, ch 1 and work a sc in each sc until the end of the row and turn your work.

Repeat this row 19 times.

FRONT PART

NEXT ROW

Ch 1 and work 2 scs in the first sc. Then, continue by working a sc in each sc till you come to the last one. Here, work 2 scs and turn your work.

NEXT TWO ROWS

Ch 1 and work a sc in each sc till the end of the row. Turn your work.

Repeat the last 3 rows 13 times more. You should end up with 42 stitches.

BACK EDGING AND SIDE TIES

ROW 1

Ch 55. With the right side of your work facing, sl st in the first chain of the foundation chain on the back. Ch 1 and work a sc in each chain. Ch 56 and turn your work.

ROW 2

Work a sl st in the second chain from the hook. Continue working a sl st in each chain until the end. Then, work a sc in each sc across the back. Then, sl st in each of the next 55 chains.

Repeat the same for the front edging and side ties.

LEG EDGING

ROW 1

With the right side of your work facing, join the yarn with a sl st to the front side edge where the tie is joined. Then, ch 1 and work a row of scs along the leg opening. Turn your work.

ROW 2

Ch 1 and work a sc in each sc till the end of the row.

Repeat the same for the other leg edging. Join the yarn with a sl st to the back side where the tie is joined.

Finally, take a piece of invisible elastic and thread it through the last row of scs at the back, front, and leg edgings.

Chapter 2 – Capri Bikini

BIKINI TOP

To begin, ch 71. Turn your work and begin the first row.

ROW 1

Work a hdc in the second chain from the hook. Continue working 1 hdc in each chain across the row. Turn your work.

ROW 2

Ch 1 and work a hdc in the next hdc from the previous row. Work 1 hdc in each hdc from the previous row till the end of the second row. Turn your work.

HOW TO CONTINUE?

Repeat this row 17 more times.

EDGE

ROW 1

To make the upper and bottom edges, ch 5, skip the next 2 hds and work a sc in the next hdc. Repeat the pattern across the row and turn your work.

ROW 2

Ch 5 and work a sc in the next chain-5 space. Repeat the pattern and turn.

ROW 3

Work a sc in the next chain-5 space. Then, when you come to the next chain-5 space, work 3 hdcs, ch1 and work 3 hdcs again in the same space. Repeat this pattern across the row.

LATERAL SIDES

ROW 1

To work the lateral sides, ch 1 and work a sc in each stitch across the row. Turn your work.

ROW 2

*Ch 2, skip the next sc and work a sc in the next sc from the previous row. Repeat the pattern across the row.

Repeat the same two rows on the other side.

TIE

Ch 350, turn and sl st in each chain.

BOTTOM

To begin, ch 45 and turn.

ROW 1

Work a hdc in the second chain from the hook. Continue working 1 hdc in each chain across the row. Turn your work. You should end up with 43 hdcs in total.

ROW 2

Ch 1 and work a hdc in each hdc from the previous row. Turn your work.

ROW 3

Work 2 hdcs together and a hdc in the next hdcs in each of the following hdcs until you come to the last two stitches. End the row with 2 hdc together. Turn your work. You should have 41 hdcs in this row.

Repeat Row 2 until you are left with 11 hdcs.

NEXT ROW

Ch 1 and then work a hdc in the next and every other hdc in the row. Turn your work.

Repeat the same row 15 more times.

NEXT ROW

Ch 1 and work 2 hdcs in the next hdc. This is an increase made. *Work a hdc in the next hdc and repeat this across the row. End the row with 2 hdcs in the last hdc.

Repeat this row until you have 65 hdcs.

NEXT ROW

Ch 1 and work a hdc in the next and every other hdc in the row. Turn your work.

Repeat the same row 4 more times.

EDGES FOR THE UPPER BACK

ROW 1

*Ch 5, skip the next 2 hdcs and work a sc in the next hdc. Repeat this pattern across the row and end the row with ch 4 and a sc in the last hdc.

ROW 2

*Ch 5 and work a sc in the next space. Repeat the pattern across the row. Turn your work.

ROW 3

*Work a sc in the next chain-5 space. Then, when you come to the next chain-5 space, work 3 hdcs, ch1 and work 3 more hdcs. Repeat the pattern across the row.

EDGES FOR THE UPPER FRONT

Join with a sl st to one corner.

NEXT ROW

Work a sc in each space and turn the work.

NEXT ROW

*Ch 5, skip the next 2 hdcs, and work a sc in the next hdc. Repeat the pattern across the row but leave the last hdc unworked. Turn your work.

NEXT ROW

Ch 5, work a sc in the next space and repeat across the row. Turn the work.

NEXT ROW

*Work a sc in the next chain-5 space, then in the next chain-5 space work 3 hdcs, ch1 and work another 3 hdcs. Repeat the pattern across the row.

SIDES & EMBROIDERY

Work a sc all around.

With a tapestry needle, embroider the top and bottom with any design you like.

Chapter 3 – Fan-Patterned Bikini

Special instructions

SC ROW

These rows begin with ch 1 and then work a sc in every stitch.

When working an increase sc row, instead of ch 1, ch 2 at the beginning of a row.

To decrease 1 sc in this sc row, work 1 sc, and then *insert the hook in the next stitch and get the yarn. Repeat the steps from* yo and pull through all the loops on the hook. Continue by working a sc in every stitch until you come to the last 3 stitches. Repeat the decrease in the next 2 stitches and work a sc in the last stitch.

DC ROW

Ch 3 and work a dc in every stitch.

To decrease a dc in each side, work a dc, *yo, insert the hook in the next stitch and grab the yarn. Yo and pull through the first two loops on the hook. Repeat the pattern from* , yo and pull through all the loops on the hook. Continue by working a dc in every stitch until you get to the last 3 stitches. Repeat the decrease in the next 2 stitches and finish the row with a dc in the last stitch.

To increase a sc in each side, work 2 scs in the first stitch. Continue by working a sc in every stitch until you come to the last stitch. Finish the row with 2 scs in the last stitch.

FAN PATTERN 1

ROW 1

Ch 1 and work a sc in the first stitch of the row. *Skip 2 stitches, work 5 dcs in the next stitch, skip 2 stitches again and work a sc in the next stitch. Repeat the pattern from* across the row. End the row with a sc in the last stitch and turn.

ROW 2

Ch 3 and work 2 dcs in the first stitch. *Work a sc in the middle dc of the group of 5 dcs and work 5 dcs in the next sc. Repeat the pattern from* across the row. End the row with a sc in the middle dc of the group of 5 dcs, and then work 3 dcs in the last sc. Turn the work.

ROW 3

Ch 1 and work a sc in the first dc in the row. *Work 5 dcs in the next stitch and then 1 sc in the middle dc from the group of 5 dcs. Repeat the pattern from* across the row. End the row with a sc in the third chain from the beginning of the previous row.

FAN PATTERN 2

ROW 1

Ch 1 and work a sc in the first stitch of the row. *Skip the first stitch, work 5 dcs in the next stitch, skip 1 stitch and work a sc in the next stitch. Repeat the pattern from* across the row. End the row with a sc in the last stitch and turn your work.

ROW 2

Ch 3 and work 2 dcs in the first stitch. *Work a sc in the middle dc of the group of 5 dcs and work 5 dcs in the next sc. Repeat the pattern from* across the row. End the row with a sc in the middle dc of the group of 5 dcs, and then work 3 dcs in the last sc. Turn the work.

ROW 3

Ch 1 and work a sc in the first dc in the row. *Work 5 dcs in the next stitch and then 1 sc in the middle dc from the group of 5 dcs. Repeat the pattern from* across the row. End the row with a sc in the third chain from the beginning of the previous row.

BOTTOM PART

Ch 55 plus 3 more to turn.

ROW 1

Work a dc in the fourth chain from the hook. Continue working a dc in every chain across the row. Turn the work.

ROW 2

This is a DC ROW.

ROW 3

Work a decrease in the DC ROW as explained in the instructions above.

ROW 4

Work another DC ROW.

ROW 5

Again, work a decrease in the DC ROW.

ROW 6

Work a DC ROW again.

ROW 7

Work a SC ROW and at the same time work a decrease on each side (read the instructions above).

NEXT 9 ROWS

Repeat Row 7 nine more times.

NEXT 6 ROWS

Decrease 1 sc on each side of the next 6 rows.

HOW TO CONTINUE?

Work SC Rows until the work measures 19 cm.

At this point, you will begin crocheting the back piece, and you will measure from here.

NEXT ROWS

Work SC rows increasing 1 sc on each side of every other row a total of 22 times and on every fourth row a total of three times.

NEXT ROWS

Work DC rows until the desired measurements.

HOW TO FINISH?

Increase 1 dc in each side of the next row and then work a DC row. Continue with DC rows until the back part measures 24 cm. Do not cut the yarn.

FAN EDGE + TIES

Work three rows following the instructions above.

Then, ch as many stitches as needed to get about 28 cm. turn and sl st in every chain and fasten the end. Cut the yarn and repeat the same to crochet another tie. Fasten this tie to the other corner of the fan edge.

Crochet the fan edge and ties for the front piece as well.

BIKINI TOP

For the top part, you will work back and forth on the chain row.

ROW 1

Ch 23 and work a sc in every chain starting from the second chain from the hook. Finish the row with 3 scs in the last chain.

Work a sc in every chain on the other side of the chain row. You should have 45 scs. Find the middle sc, mark it with a stitch marker and turn.

ROW 2

Work a sc in every sc across the row paying attention to work 3 scs in the middle sc.

NEXT 5 ROWS

Repeat the same as in Row 2.

NEXT 3 ROWS

Work DC rows but doing 3 dcs in the middle stitch.

In the last DC stitch, work 5 dcs in the middle stitch. At the same time, increase 2 stitches in the last row. The number of stitches you get can be divided by 4+1.

NEXT ROW

Work the same row as the first row in the Fan pattern 2 (read the instructions above). Mark the middle stitch with a stitch marker.

NEXT ROW

Work the same row as Row 2 in the Fan pattern 2 but instead of 5 dcs, work 5 dcs, ch 1 and work 5 more dcs.

NEXT ROW

This row is the same as Row 3 for the Fan pattern 2. When you come to the top chain of the previous row, work 5 dcs and fasten off.

Repeat the same to crochet the other cup.

FAN EDGE AND TIES ON THE SIDE

ROW 1

Ch as many stitches as needed to get about 37 cm.

Continue to work along the bottom edge of the cup. Work in the front loop from the right side. Work 34 stitches. Then, ch stitches to get about 2 cm and work 34 sc along the bottom edge of the other cup.

Ch for about 37 cm and turn.

ROW 2

Work a sc in each stitch across the row and turn.

ROW 3

Sl st in every stitch and fasten off.

TIES

Ch for about 48 cm and turn. Work a sl st in every chain. When you come to the

5 dcs on top of the cup, work a sl st in the middle dc.

Turn and work a sl st in the same stitch and continue to work a sl st in every chain on the other side of the row. Fasten off and then repeat the same for the other cup.

Chapter 4 – Square-Patterned Bikini Top

For this bikini, you will need 5 different colors. You will create three squares that are then sewn together.

SQUARES

To begin, ch 5 and sl st to join into a ring.

ROW 1

Continue using the same color. Ch 3 and work 7 dcs in the ring. Finish the row with a sl st in the chain-3 and cut the yarn. Turn the piece.

ROW 2

Use color 2. Ch 3 and work a dc in the first dc from the previous row. In each of the remaining dcs from the first row, work 2 dcs. When you come to the end of the row, finish with a sl st at the beginning of the row. *i.e.* in the chain-3. Cut the yarn and turn.

ROW 3

Use color 3. Ch 3 and work a dc in the first dc from the previous row. Again, work a dc in the next dc. Continue working in each dc from the previous row alternating between 2 dcs and 1 dc. When you come to the end, sl st into the beginning chain-3. Cut the yarn and turn the work.

ROW 4

Use color 4

Ch 7 and work a dc in the first dc from the previous row. Then, *work a dc in each of the following 6 dcs from the previous row, ch 4 and work a dc in the last of the 6 dcs. Repeat the pattern from* two more times. You will have 5 more dcs left from the previous row. Work a dc in each of these and finish the row with a sl st. cut the yarn and turn the piece.

ROW 5

Use color 5. Ch 3 and work a dc in the first stitch. In each of the next 6 dcs, work a dc. Then, *work 3 dcs in the chain-loop space, then ch 3 and work 3 more dcs in the same space. Work a dc in each of the following 7 dcs.

Repeat the pattern from * across the row and finish with a sl st in the beginning chain-3 space. Cut the yarn.

If you need a smaller size, do not work row 5. On the other hand, if you need a bigger size, work row 5 once again.

Repeat this procedure to make 6 squares in total.

To make one cup, sew three squares together (edge to edge) so that they form a triangle.

TIES

Work with two strands and make three chains, two should be about 120 cm and the other 15 cm long. Sew a bead to the ends of the cords. Use the shorter strand to tie the cups at the center front. Thread one longer strand through the tops of the cups. You will tie this one behind the neck. Thread the other longer strand at the sides of the cups and this will be tied at the back.

Chapter 5 – Tripoli Bikini

Special instructions

To decrease in a SC row, work a sc, *insert the hook in the next stitch and grab the yarn. Repeat the pattern from* , yo and pull through 3 loops on the hook. Work a sc in every stitch. When you come to the last 3 stitches, repeat the decrease again in 2 stitches, and work a sc in the last one.

To increase, work 2 stitches in the first and last stitch of the row.

FAN PATTERN

ROW 1

Ch 1 and work a sc in the first stitch of the row. *Skip the first stitch, work 5 dcs in the next stitch, skip 1 stitch and work a sc in the next stitch. Repeat the pattern from* across the row. End the row with a sc in the last stitch and turn your work.

ROW 2

Ch 3 and work 2 dcs in the first stitch. *Work a sc in the middle dc of the group of 5 dcs and work 5 dcs in the next sc. Repeat the pattern from* across the row. End the row with a sc in the middle dc of the group of 5 dcs, and then work 3 dcs in the last sc. Turn the work.

ROW 3

Ch 1 and work a sc in the first dc in the row. *Work 5 dcs in the next stitch and then 1 sc in the middle dc from the group of 5 dcs. Repeat the pattern from* across the row. End the row with a sc in the third chain from the beginning of the previous row.

BOTTOM PART

You will work the bottom part by starting at the top of the front piece until you reach the top of the back piece.

To begin, chain 45.

ROW 1

Begin by working a sc in the third chain from the hook and continue working 1 sc in each chain until the end of the row. You should now have 43 scs in this row. This is a SC row.

This number of stitches can be divided by 6+1. Turn your work.

ROW 2

Work the same row back and forth once again.

HOW TO CONTINUE?

Work SC rows with a decrease in every other row a total of 15 times. After this, you should have 13 scs.

Work these rows back and forth with 1 sc in every sc until the piece measures 19 cm. Continue measuring the work from this point.

NEXT ROWS

You will now start an increase (read the instructions above).

Repeat this in every other row a total of three times and then on every row a total of 8 times. Again, repeat the increase again in every other row a total of 13 times.

Remember that the final number of stitches can be divided by 6+1.

Continue working SC rows until the work measures 23 cm. Do not cut the yarn.

FAN EDGE AND TIES

Work the rows 1-3 of the Fan pattern (read the instructions above).

NEXT ROWS

Ch 2 and work a sc in the first chain worked. *Ch 1 again, and work 1 sc in the previous sc. Repeat the pattern from* until the tie measures approx. 30-40 cm. Fasten off and repeat the same steps to create another tie. Fasten it off on the other side of the fan edge.

Repeat the same procedure for the front piece.

BIKINI TOP

Begin by ch 3 and forming a ring with a sl st in the first chain.

ROW 1

Ch 1 and work a sc in the first chain in the ring. Then, work 2 scs in each of the following 2 chains in the ring. You should now have 6 sc. Attach a stitch marker and work in the round.

ROW 2

Work 2 scs in the first sc and repeat the same in the next sc. Ch 1 and repeat the pattern from the beginning of the row. You should have 4 sc with 1 ch in between.

ROW 3

Work 1 sc in the first sc and repeat this in the next 3 scs. In the next chain, work 1 sc and ch 1 (this will make a corner) and 1 sc. Repeat the pattern a total of 3 times. So, you should now have 3 corners with 6 scs between each corner.

ROW 4

Work a sc in every sc. When you come to the chain in the corners, work 1 sc, ch 1 and 1 sc. Now, you should have 8 scs between each corner.

ROW 5

Work a sc in every sc from the previous row. In every corner, work a sc, ch 1 and another sc. Now, there should be 10 sc separating each corner.

Continue working in the same manner and increasing until the piece measures the desired size.

LAST ROW

As in the previous rows, work with scs and increase along 2 of the sides including all the corners. Along the last side, work a hdc in the first stitch. Then, *ch 1, skip one sc and then work a hdc in the next stitch.

Repeat the pattern from * until you reach the corner. Here, sl st in the first chain from the beginning of the round (eyelet holes). Repeat the same process to create another cup.

TIES

Begin with ch 2 and work a sc in the first chain worked. Then, *ch 1 and work a sc in the previous sc. Repeat the pattern from* until the tie measures about 110 cm. Fasten off and thread the tie through the eyelet holes on both bikini parts.

Repeat the same to create another tie.

Chapter 6 – Safari Bikini

BIKINI TOP

Begin with ch 8 and turn.

ROW 1

Work a dc into the second chain from the hook. Then, continue working 1 dc in each of the remaining 6 chains. Turn.

ROW 2

Work a dc in each dc till the end of the row. Continue repeating this row until the piece measures 6 cm. Use a stitch marker to mark this last row.

NEXT ROW

Work a dc in each dc and when you come to the corner, work 4 dcs here and then 8 dcs down and along the other side. You will have 20 dcs in the row. Turn your work.

NEXT ROWS

Work a dc in each dc until the piece measures 10 cm from the row you have marked with the stitch marker.

It is important to check how much the piece measures because once it reaches 3 cm from the marked row, you should increase 1 dc at one side of the piece on every 3 cm a total of 3 times.

To increase, work one extra dc into the second outermost dc from the side. When you reach the last row, the piece should measure about 16 cm from the center front and out towards the side.

Repeat the same steps to create another piece for the bikini top.

HOW TO ASSEMBLE?

To assemble the pieces, you will have to work a row around the whole bikini edge starting from the wrong side. You will also need to begin from the bottom corner of one of the pieces.

Work a sl st into the first stitch and then work a dc into each dc-row along the whole bottom edge and the other edges of the bikini. This is how the two pieces are held together.

To finish, create a row of laces on the top of the bikini.

Ch 4, *skip the first stitch and work a tr in the next stitch and then ch 1. Repeat the pattern from* until you come to the last stitch. Here, work a tr and turn.

NEXT ROW

Ch 1, work a dc into the first tr and then work a dc around the chain. Work a dc into the next tr and repeat this pattern along the edge.

TIES

You will need to create a string from each side of the bikini.

Work a sl st into the corner of the bikini part. Ch 70 (or the length you need), turn and work a dc into the second chain from the hook. Continue working a dc into each chain and when you some to the end, sl st in the sl st from the beginning.

BOTTOM PART

NOTE: To bind off, turn the work when the number of dcs left in the row equals the number of stitches to be bound off. Then, you can begin the next row.

To increase at the end of a row, work a number of chains that is equal to the number of increases + 1 extra chain. Turn and work a dc into the second chain and continue working a dc into each chain.

Begin with ch 89.

ROW 1

Ch 4, *skip the first stitch and work a tr in the next stitch, ch 1 and repeat the pattern from* . When you come to the end of the row, work a tr.

ROW 2

Work a dc into each stitch. Continue repeating this row until the piece measures 10-11 cm. Bind off at the end of each row (read the instructions above). So, you should have 9 sts 2 times, 4 sts 2 times, 2 sts once and 1 st 9 times. This equals 14 dcs left in the row.

At this point, the piece should be about 21-25 cm. Mark this row with a stitch marker.

Continue working in the same manner until the piece measures 8 cm from the marked row. Then, increase each side at the end of the row (read the instructions above). So, you should have 1 st once, 2 sts 4 times, 3sts 4 times and 2 sts 8 times. This equals 88 dcs.

Continue working rows of dcs until the peace is about 30 cm from the marked row.

NEXT ROW

Ch 4, *skip the first stitch, work a tr in the next stitch and ch 1. Repeat the pattern from* and end the row with a tr.

For the final row, work a dc into each stitch.

HOW TO FINISH?

You should now crochet around a leg opening. Work a dc, *ch 1, skip one stitch and work a dc into the next stitch. Repeat the pattern from* across the row. You should begin from the right side of the front piece, and work down and along the side and then around the leg opening and up along the back piece.

Repeat the same on the other side.

Do not crochet along the top edge of the back and front piece. Here, you can thread a piece of leather or invisible elastic so that the width of the bottom part can be adjusted.

Chapter 7 – Adria Bikini

BIKINI TOP

ROW 1

Ch 13 and work a sc in the second chain from the hook. Work a sc in the remaining chains.

NEXT ROWS

Ch 1, turn the work and work a sc in each stitch across the row until you reach the middle sc. Work 3 scs and then sc across each stitch back.

Repeat as many rows as necessary to get the desired size.

EDGE

Do not fasten off. With the right side facing, on both upper sides, work a hdc, ch 2 and skip 1 space across till the end on the bottom side.

LAST ROW & TIES

In every chain-2 space, work a sc and 1 picot. Repeat this until you come to the middle chain-2 space. Here you will need to make a neck strap or tie. So, ch 70 and work a row of sc and then back. Again, work 1 sc and 1 picot in every chain-2 space and on the bottom side, work hdc, ch 2 and skip 1 dc across till the end of the row.

To make the second piece repeat the same procedure.

To make the bottom tie, ch as many stitches as needed to for the tie to be about 120 cm long and work a row of sc in each chain. Thread the bottom strap through the bottom chain-2 spaces and weave in any loose ends.

BOTTOM PART

ROW 1

Ch 15 and work a sc in the third chain from the hook. Continue working a sc in each stitch across.

NEXT ROWS

This is the increase row where you have to increase on both sides (work 2 scs in one stitch). Then, you will increase 4 times in every fourth row and then again in every second row till you get the size you need.

LAST ROW FOR THE BACK PART

Work a hdc, ch 2 and skip 1 sc. Repeat the pattern across the row and fasten off.

You will now continue working on the front part.

Facing the right side, join the yarn with a sl st and crochet scs until the work measures 7 cm without increases.

Then, increase on both sides in every second row 18 times till you get the front size that you need. To make the slips bigger, add more rows both to the front and back and keep increasing in the same manner.

LAST ROW

Work a hdc, ch 2 and skip 1 sc. Repeat this pattern across the row.

EDGE

To make an edge on both sides of the bottom part, work a row of evenly spaced scs.

In both corners make ties. Ch 70-80 and work scs back till you reach the beginning, and in both upper sides in every chain-2 space work 1 sc and 1 picot.

Chapter 8 – Vintage Bikini

Special instructions

Grid pattern – Ch 2, skip a stitch and work a dc into the next stitch.

BOTTOM PART

You should begin crocheting the bottom piece from the front. Ch 97, ch 3 more and turn.

ROW 1

Work a tr into the fourth chain, ch 1, skip one chain and work a tr into the next chain. Repeat the pattern across the row.

ROW 2

Work a tr into the first tr. Pay attention to insert the hook under 3 strands, *i.e.* into the main part of the tr. Ch 1 and repeat the pattern across the row.

ROWS 3, 4, 5

These rows are the same as row 2. You should now have 49 trs.

NEXT ROWS

Work rows of dcs in the following manner. Work a dc into a tr and then 1 dc into the chain. You should have 97 dcs. Repeat this row about 12 times or until the piece measures 7cm.

Then, you will need to decrease at each end of the rows to follow. To decrease, follow this pattern.

Work 14 dcs once, then 3 dcs once and 1 dc 17 times. Then, you will have to decrease 1 dc at each end of the following 6 rows. You will have 17 dscs remaining. Continue straight for 5 cm.

When you start working the back, you will have to increase 1 dc at each end of the following 19 alternative rows. Then, increase at each end of every following row following this pattern: work a dc four times, then 2 dcs 7 times, and 3 dcs once. You should now have 97 dcs remaining.

NEXT ROW

Work a dc in every stitch across the row.

NEXT 12 ROWS

Continue working a dc row without increasing.

NEXT 3 ROWS

Working in dc, decrease 8 dcs at each end.

NEXT ROW

Still working in dc, decrease 10 dcs at each end. You should have 28 dcs remaining.

NEXT ROW

Work a dc in every stitch across the row.

NEXT ROW

Now, you will work in another pattern. You will work in dc but from left to right. In the first row of this pattern, you will have to miss 1 dc between each tr 49 tr. Fasten off after the 59th row.

To assemble, stitch side seams and work 1 row of the grid pattern – dc from left to right – around the leg openings.

Make two ties and thread them through the first row of grids and tie at the side.

BIKINI TOP

Ch 33 plus 1 more and turn.

ROW 1

Work a dc in every chain across the row.

ROW 2 + NEXT ROWS

This is also a dc row, but this time you will work 3 dcs into the center stitch on every third row 6 times. At the same time, decrease 1 dc at each end of every third row 6 times. Continue decreasing 1 dc at each end of the following 5 alternate rows. Then, decrease 1 dc at each end of the following 11 rows.

To crochet the second cup, repeat the same process.

HOW TO ASSEMBLE?

ROW 1

Work dc in every stitch across the row.

ROWS 2 & 3

Work along the two edges of the cups creating the grid pattern. To join the cups, overlap the two rows of grids at the center placing the right side over the left.

To create the base, ch 60 and work a row of dc along the lower edge of the two cups. Again, ch 60 and work 3 rows of grids across these stitches.

NECK BAND

Ch 110 and work 2 rows of grids. Stitch the ends of the neck band to the top of the cups.

Chapter 9 – Halter Top Bikini

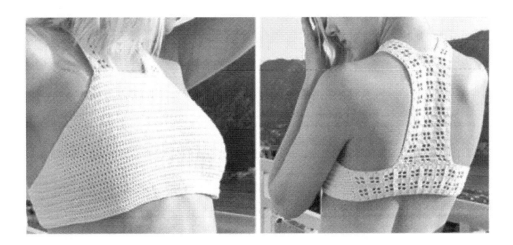

THE FRONT PART

ROW 1

Ch 41 and work a dc in each chain starting from the third chain from the hook.

ROWS 2-26

Ch 2, turn your work and work 2 dcs in the sam space, then, work a dc in each dc from the previous row until you come to the last dc. Here, work 3 dcs.

ROWS 27-36

Ch 2 and turn the work. Work a dc in each dc across the row.

THE BACK HORIZONTAL STRIPE

ROW 1

Ch 3 and work a dc in the following 21 dcs.

ROW 2

Ch 3 and work a dc in the next 3 dcs. *ch 2, skip 2 dcs and work a dc in the next dc. Ch 2 again, skip 2 dcs and work a dc in each of the next 4 dcs. Repeat the pattern from* once.

ROW 3

Ch 3, work a dc in the next 3 dcs. *ch 2, work a dc in the next dc, ch 2 and work a dc in each of the next 4 dcs. Repeat this pattern from* once.

Repeat the pattern of row 1-3 9 times and then repeat Row 1. Using a sl st, join the stripe to the opposite side.

BACK VERTICAL STRIPE

Work 31 dc in the middle of the stripe.

ROW 1

Ch 3 and work a dc in each of the following 3 dcs. *Ch 2, skip 2 dcs, and work a dc in the next dc. Ch 2 again, skip 2 dcs and work a dcs in each of the next 4 dcs. Repeat this pattern twice.

ROW 2

Begin the row as the previous one. *Ch 2, work a dc in the next dc, ch 2 and work a dc in each of the following 4 dcs. Repeat the pattern from * two times.

ROW 3

Ch 3 and work a dc across the row.

Repeat the pattern of rows 1-3 eight times.

FRONT STRIPES

ROW 1

Ch 3 and work a dc in each of the next 3 dcs. Ch 2, skip 2 dcs and work a dc in the next dc. Ch 2 again, skip 2 and work a dc in the next 4 dcs.

ROW 2

Ch 3 and work a dc in each of the next 3 dcs. *Ch 2, work a dc in the next dc, ch 2 and work a dc in each of the next 4 dcs.

ROW 3

Ch 3 and work a dc across the row.

Repeat the pattern of rows 1-3 seven times Use a sl st to join the stripes to the front part.

Chapter 10 – Budapest Bikini Top

To begin, chain as many stitches as needed to reach from one side of your ribs to another.

ROW 1-6

Sc across the row starting from the very first chain. When you come to the end, ch 1 and turn.

ROW 7

Work a sc in the first stitch. Skip the next one and go into the next stitch. Repeat this pattern across the row.

Repeat Row 7 until you get the shape and measure you need.

TOP DESIGN

ROW 1

Work a sc with no ch 1. Skip 2 stitches and create a tr into the third stitch. Continue working trs skipping 1 stitch in between.

ROW 2

Ch 1 and tr in the very first stitch. Skip the second tr and create a tr in the next one. Continue working a tr in each space.

Continue repeating this row until the pattern reaches the measure you need. Do not cut off yet.

NECK STRAPS

Chain as many stitches as you need and then cut off. To create the second strap, attach the yarn to the stitch you want your strap to be and chain from there.

BACK STRAPS

Create the back straps in the same way as the neck straps.

Conclusion

It's already the end. Hopefully, you have picked a pattern to instruct you on how to crochet THE bikini for this summer. The book has revealed to you 10 sexy bikini patterns that you can try out and show off when relaxing on the beach on those hot days that are to come.

Besides that, the book also gives you a quick method of blocking your projects, *i.e.* letting the patterns open up. The projects can be done really quickly, so saying that you don't have time for something like this is not an excuse.

Hope you've had fun with this book and found the patterns as amazing as I do.

Summer Crochet
10 Appealing Projects Of Crochet Pareo And Wraps

Introduction

Some time ago, when someone would mention crochet, I would think about my grandmother sitting in the garden and crocheting shawls and mittens. It seemed to me that crochet is a perfect pastime for all of our grannies. However, I soon discovered how trendy crochet projects can be, and I was amazed by the galore of all those projects we can crochet.

Crochet is apparently not only for killing time during long winter nights. You can make use of a variety of yarns, hooks, and stitch combinations and crochet wonderful pieces. This time, I prepared for you crochet summer wrap and pareo patterns. As with any other crochet project, you will need to know the basics – single crochet, double crochet, treble crochet, and slip stitch. And that's it! Just follow the steps to arrange these stitches, and you'll get trendy accessories for this summer.

I know you can't wait to try out your projects once you finish them. However, to allow the patterns to fully show up, you need to block your works. One quick and simple way to do it is to use your iron. Just put a damp towel over your piece of work and press the iron over the towel. Make quick motions so that you steam your wraps. In just a few minutes you will be able to wrap yourself up in your summer wraps and pareo.

Chapter 1 – Pineapple Summer Wrap

Yarn: 6 balls

Special instructions:

SHELL ROW: Begin with ch and shell in the ch-2 space of the first shell

INCREASE-SHELL ROW: Ch 4 and work an increase-shell in the ch-2 space of the first shell.

REPEAT PATTERN 1: Ch 3 and work a sc in the next ch-3 space.

SHELL = Work (2 dcs, ch 2, 2 dcs) in the indicated stitch or ch-space.

INCREASE-SHELL = Work (2 dcs, [ch 2, dc] twice, ch 2, 2 dcs) in the indicated chain-space.

NOTE: Work in stitches and ch-spaces indicated only, skip all other stitches and ch-spaces.

Begin by chaining 30.

ROW 1

Start from the 5th chain from the hook. Work a shell here and ch 2. Skip 3 chains and work a sc in the next one. *Ch 3 and work a sc in the third chain. Repeat the pattern from* 4 more times.

Then, ch 2 and work a shell in the 4th chain. Ch 1, skip one and work a dc in the last chain in the row.

Turn your work. You should have 2 shells in the row, 5 ch-3 and 2 ch-2 spaces.

ROW 2

Begin by chaining 4 and go to the first ch-2 space of the first shell. Here, work an increase-shell. Ch 2 and skip the next ch-2 space. You come to the ch-3 space; here work a sc.

Ch 3 and work a sc in a ch-3 space. Repeat the pattern from 3 more times.

Now you come to a ch-2 space of the last shell. Ch 2 and work an increase-shell.

Finish the row by chaining 1 and working a dc in the 3rd chain of the turning chain. Turn your work.

ROW 3

Star the row with ch 4 and find the first ch-2 space of the increase-shell from the previous row. Work a shell here. Then, in the next ch-2 space work a dc, ch 2 and work another dc. In the next ch-2 space work a shell and then ch 2. Skip the next ch-2 space and work a sc in the ch-3 space.

Ch 3 and work a sc in the next ch-3 space. Repeat the pattern from 2 more times.

Ch 2 and work a shell in the first ch-2 space of the next increase-shell. When you come to the next ch-2 space, work a dc, ch 2 and work another dc.

End the row by working a shell in the last ch-2 space. Ch 1 and work a dc in the 3rd chain of the turning chain. Turn your work.

ROW 4

Start the row with ch 4. Now you come to the first shell from the previous row. Find the ch-2 space and work a shell here. Ch 1 and work 9 dcs in the ch-2 space. Then, ch 1 again and work a shell in the ch-space of the next shell.

Ch 2 and skip a ch-2 space. Then, you come to the ch-3 space; work a sc here.

Ch 3 and work a sc in the ch-3 space. Repeat the pattern from once again.

Ch 2 and since you will have to skip the ch-2 space, go into the ch-2 space of the next shell. Work a shell here and ch 1. Continue by working 9 dcs in the next ch-2 space. Ch 1 again and work a shell in the ch-2 space of the next shell. Ch 1 once again and finish the row by working a dc in the 3rd chain of the turning chain.

Turn your work.

ROW 5

Ch 4 and work a shell in the ch-2 space of the first shell from the previous row.

To begin the repeat pattern for this row, *ch 2 and find the first dc from the group of 9 dcs. Work a sc here.* *Ch 3 and work a sc in the next dc**. Repeat the pattern from * to * 7 more times.

Ch 2 and work a shell in the ch-2 space of the next shell*.

Ch 2 again and work a sc in the next ch-3 space (you will have to skip one ch-2 space). Ch 3 and work a sc in the next ch-3 space. Now, ch 2 and work a shell in the ch-2 space of the next shell (you will have to skip one ch-2 space).

Repeat the pattern from *to* once.

End the row by chaining 1 and working a dc in the 3rd chain of the turning chain. Turn your work.

ROW 6

Ch 4 and work a shell in the ch-2 space.

Begin the repeat pattern by chaining 3. Work a sc in the ch-3 space (you will need to skip one ch-2 space). Then, *ch 3 and work a sc in the next ch-3 space.** *Repeat the pattern from* * *to* * *6 more times. Ch 3 and work a shell in the ch-2 space of the next shell.**

Ch 2 and work a sc in the ch-3 space (you will need to skip one ch-2 space). Ch 2 again and skip another ch-2 space. Now, you come to the ch-2 space of the next shell. Work a shell here.

Repeat the pattern from *to* .

End the row by chaining 1 and working a dc in the 3rd chain of the turning chain. Turn your work.

ROW 7

As the previous rows, begin this row by chaining 4. Work a shell in the ch-2 space.

Ch 3 and work a sc in the second ch-3 space. *Ch 3 and work a sc in the next ch-3 space.** Repeat the pattern from * *to* * 5 more times.

Ch 3 and work a shell in the ch-2 space of the next shell.*

Continue by chaining 1 and working a shell in the ch-2 space of the next shell.

Repeat the pattern from *to* and then ch 1. End the row by chaining 1 and working a dc in the 3rd chain of the turning chain.

Turn your work.

ROW 8

Ch 4 and work a shell in the first ch-2 space.

Ch 3 and work a sc in the second ch-3 space (you will need to skip one ch-3 space). *Ch 3 and work a sc in the next ch-3 space** and repeat the pattern from * *to* * four more times.

Ch 3 again and work a shell in the ch-2 space of the next shell.*

You will now come to the ch-1 space. Work a shell here and then again a shell in the ch-2 space. Repeat the pattern from *to* .

To end the row, ch 1 and work a dc in the 3rd chain of the turning chain. Turn your work.

ROW 9

Ch 4 and begin this row by working an increase shell in the ch-2 space of the first shell.

Ch 3 and work a sc in the second ch-3 space. *Ch 3 and work a sc in the next ch-3 space.** Repeat the pattern from * *to* * 3 more times.*

Work a shell in the ch-2 space of the next shell and ch 1. Work another shell in the next ch-2 space and ch 1 again, and another shell in the next ch-2 space.

Repeat the pattern from *to* . Now, you will come to the last shell in the row. Work an increase-shell in the ch-2 space of the last shell.

Finish the row by chaining 1 and working a dc in the 3rd chain of the turning chain. Trn your work.

ROW 10

Begin by chaining 4 and working a shell in the ch-2 space. When you come to the next ch-2 space, work a dc, ch 2 and another dc. For the next ch-2 space, do a shell.

*Ch 3 and work a sc in the second ch-3 space (you will have to skip one ch-3 space). *Ch 3 and work a sc in the next ch-3 space.** repeat the pattern from * to * two more times and ch 3.*

Work a shell in the ch-2 space of the next shell and repeat that once again.

Then, work a shell in the ch-2 space of the next shell. Repeat the pattern from *to* and work a shell in the ch-2 space. In the next ch-2 space, work a dc, ch 2 and work another dc.

In the last ch-2 space in the row, work a shell and ch 1. End the row with dc in the 3rd chain of the turning chain. Turn your work.

ROW 11

Ch 4 and work a shell in the first ch-2 space. Ch 1 and go into the next ch-2 space and work 9 dcs here. Ch 1 again and work a shell in the next ch-2 space.

*Ch 2 and work a sc in the second ch-3 space (skip one). *Ch 3 and work a sc in the next ch-3 space** and repeat this once again.

Ch 2 and skip one ch-3 space. Work a shell in the next ch-2 space and then ch 1. In the next ch-2 space, work 9 dcs and ch 1. Work a shell in the ch-2 space and repeat the pattern from * across the row.

Ch 1 and finish the row with a dc in the 3rd chain of the turning chain. Turn your work.

ROW 12

Ch 4 and work a shell in the ch-2 space.

*Ch 2 and work a sc in the first dc of the group of 9 dcs. Then, **ch 3 and work a sc in the next dc.** Repeat this 8 times. Ch 2 and work a shell in the ch-2 space of the next shell. *** Ch 2 and work a sc in the ch-3 space (you will have to skip one ch-2 space). Then, ch 3 and work a sc in the next ch-3 space.

Ch 2 and work a shell in the second ch-2 space (skip one). Repeat the pattern from *across the row. End the row at **. Finish the row as the previous ones.

ROW 13

Ch 4 and work a shell in the ch-2 space. *Ch 3 and work a sc in the ch-3 space (skip one ch-2 space). *Ch 3 and sc in the next ch-3 space** Repeat this 7 times.

Ch 3 and work a shell in the ch-2 space of the next shell. ***Ch 2 and work a sc in the ch-3 space (skip one ch-2 space). Ch 2 and work a shell in the second ch-2 space (skip one ch-2 space). Repeat the pattern from *across the row and end at* **. Finish the row as the previous ones.

ROW 14

Ch 4 and work a shell in the ch-2 space of the first shell.

Ch 3 and work a sc in the second ch-3 space (skip one ch-3 space). *Ch 3 and sc in the next ch-3 space** 6 times.

Ch 3 and wk a shell in the ch-2 space of the next shell.***Ch 1 and work a shell in the ch-2 space of the next shell. Repeat the pattern from *across the row and end at* **. Finish the row as he previous ones.

ROW 15

Ch 4 and work a shell in the ch-2 space.

Ch 3 and work a sc in the second ch-3 space (skip one). *Ch 3 and sc in ch-3 space** 5 times Ch 3 and work a shell in the ch-2 space of the next space.

***Work a shell in the next ch-1 space and then work a shell in the ch-2 space of the next shell. Repeat the pattern from *across the row and end at* *. Finish the row as the previous ones.

ROW 16

Ch 4 and work an increase-shell in the ch-2 space of the first shell.

Ch 3 and work a sc in the second ch-3 space. *Ch 3 and work a sc in the next ch-3 space 4 times. Ch 3. **[shell in ch-2 space of next shell, ch1] twice. Work a shell in the next ch-2 space. Repeat the pattern from *across the row and end at* *. Work an increase shell in the ch-2 space of the last shell.

End the row in the same way as the previous ones.

ROW 17

Ch 4 and work a shell in the first ch-2 space. In the next ch-2 space, work a dc, ch 2 and work another dc.

Then, work a shell in the next ch-2 space.

Ch 3 and work a sc in the second ch-3 space. *Ch 3 and work a sc in next ch-3 space 3 times and ch 3. ** Work the following sequence twice: shell in ch-2 space of the next shell and ch 2.

Work a shell in the next ch-2 space and repeat the pattern from *across the row and end at* *.

Work a shell in the ch-2 space, then work a dc, ch 2 and work another dc in the next ch-2 space.

In the last ch-2 space work a shell. Finish the row as the previous ones.

ROWS 18-45

Repeat the rows from 11 to 17 four more times.

ROWS 56-50

Repeat the rows 11-15.

EDGE

Ch 4 and work a shell in the first ch-2 space. *Ch 2 and work a shell in the second ch-3 space. *Ch 2 and work a shell in the second ch-3 space.** Repeat the pattern from * to * once again.**

Ch 2 and work a shell in the ch-2 space of the next shell. Repeat this pattern 2 more times.

Repeat the pattern from *across the row and end at* **.

Ch 2 and work a shell in the ch-2 space of the last shell.

End the row in the same manner as the previous ones. Fasten off. Weave in ends and add fringes.

Chapter 2 – Flower Wrap

Begin by chaining 256.

ROW 1

Go into the 6th chain from the hook and work a dc. This will count as the first mesh stitch.

Ch 1 and work a dc in the second stitch. Repeat the pattern from across the row. You should have 121 mesh stitches.

ROW 2

This is a decrease row. So, you will have to decrease one mesh stitch at each side.

Work a sl st in the first ch-1 space. Work a sl st in the next dc as well. Then, ch 4 and this will count as the first mesh stitch in this row.

Work a dc in the next dc and ch 1. Repeat the pattern from across the row. When you come to the last mesh stitch, turn your work and leave the stitch unworked.

You should end the row with 119 mesh stitches.

ROW 3, *etc.*

All the rows to follow are the same as ROW 2. Continue decreasing 2 mesh stitches until you are left with only one mesh stitch.

EDGE

ROW 1

Ch 1 and work a sc in the same stitch. Work sc evenly across the row. In the remaining 2 corners, work 3 scs. To end this row, work 2 scs in the same stitch (as you did at the beginning of this row). Join with a slip stitch to the first stitch.

ROW 2

Work a row of reverse single crochet and fasten off.

CROCHET FLOWERS

FLOWER 1

Begin by chaining 4 and join with a sl st to form a ring.

ROW 1

Ch 1 and *work a sc in the ring. Ch 6 and repeat the pattern from* 7 more times. End the row by joining with sl st to the first stitch in the row. You should now have 8 ch-6 places.

ROW 2

Ch 4 and in the first ch-6 space work 3 trs, then ch 4 and work a sl st. *In the next ch-6 space work a sl st. Ch 4 and work 3 trs, ch 4 and work a sl st in the next ch-6 space. Repeat the pattern from* across the row. The flower should have 8 petals.

FLOWER 2

Begin by chaining 4. Join with a sl st to form a ring.

ROW 1

Ch 1 and work 12 scs in the ring. Then, join with a sl st to the first sc in the row.

ROW 2

Ch 6, and this will count as 1 dc + ch 6.

Skip one sc and work a dc in the next. Then, ch 3. Repeat the pattern from across the row and join with a sl st. In this row, you should have 6 dc and ch-3 spaces.

ROW 3

In each ch-3 space from the previous row, work a sc, 2 dcs, tr, 2 dcs and a sc. T end the row, join with a sl st and fasten off. The flower should have 6 petals.

Add the fringes. For one fringe, you will need 3 strands about 12 inches long. Hold them together and fold in half. With a hook, insert the fringes into the wrap stitches.

Chapter 3 – Solomon's Knot Wrap

Yarn – 8 balls

Special instructions:

SK = Solomon's knot

HSK = half Solomon's knot

Begin by chaining 2.

ROW 1

In the second chain from the hook, work a sc and then ch 1. Work another sc into the same stitch. Turn your work.

ROW 2

Ch 1 and work a sc in the first sc from the previous row. Ch 3 and skip the next ch-1 space. End the row with a sc in the next sc. Turn your work.

ROW 3

Ch 1 and work 2 scs in the first stitch. Then, ch 3 and skip the ch-3 space. In the last stitch work 2 scs and turn the work.

ROW 4

Ch 1 and work a sc in the first stitch. Repeat the pattern from once again. Then, ch and skip the ch-3 space. Work a sc in the next stitch and ch 1. In the last stitch, work a sc and turn the work.

ROW 5

Ch 1 and work a sc in the first stitch. Ch 2 and skip the ch-1 space. Then, work a sc in the next stitch and ch 3. Again, skip the ch-3 space and work a sc in the next stitch.

Ch 2 and mix another ch-1 space. In the last stitch, work a sc and turn the work.

ROW 6

As in the previous rows, ch 1 and work a sc in the first stitch. Then, ch 3 and skip the ch-2 space. Work a sc in the next stitch and ch 3. Skip the ch-3 space and go into the next stitch and work a sc. Skip the ch-2 space and work a sc in the last one. Turn your work.

ROW 7

Ch 1 and work 2 scs in the first stitch. *Ch 3 and skip the ch-3 space. Then, work a sc in the next stitch. Repeat the pattern from* across the row. When you come to the last stitch, work 2 scs. Turn your work.

ROW 8

Ch 1 and work a sc in the first stitch. Ch 1 again and work another sc in the next stitch. *Ch 3 and skip the ch-3 space. Work a sc in the next stitch. Repeat the pattern from* across the row. In the last stitch, ch 1 and work a sc. Turn your work.

ROW 9

Begin by chaining 1 and working a sc in the first stitch. Ch 2 and skip the ch-1 space. Work a sc in the next stitch.

Ch 3 and skip the ch-3 space. Work a sc in the next stitch and repeat the pattern from across the stitch. When you come to the end of the row, ch 2 and skip the ch-1 space. In the last stitch, work a sc. Turn your work.

ROW 10

Similarly to the previous rows, ch 1 and work a sc in the first sc. Continue by chaining 3 and skipping the ch-2 space. Work a sc in the next stitch, *Ch 3 and skip the ch-3 space. Then, work a sc in the next stitch. Repeat the pattern from* across the row. End the row by chaining 3 and missing the ch-2 space. Work a sc in the last stitch and turn the work.

ROW 11, *etc.*

Repeat the same pattern from the ROW 7 to ROW 10 22 more times.

EDGE

ROW 1

Ch 1 and work scs evenly across the down edge. When you come to the corner, work 3 scs here. Continue by working scs evenly across the other side. Turn your work. In this row, you should have 98 scs, 3 scs in the corner and 98 scs on the other side.

ROW 2

Ch 1 and work a sc in the first 99 scs from the previous row. Then, work 3 scs in the next stitch and continue by working a sc in each of the following 99 scs. Turn your work.

ROW 3

Ch 1 and work a sc in each of the following 100 scs. In the next one, work 3 scs and then repeat the pattern from the beginning of the row. Turn your work.

ROW 4

Ch 1 and work a sc in the first stitch. Then work 1 HSK and then 1 SK. Skip the next stitch and work a sc in the next one.

Work 2 SKs and skip the following 5 scs. Work a sc in the next stitch. Repeat the patterns from 15 more times.

**Skip the next 2 scs and then work 2 SKs. Work a sc in the next stitch. Repeat the pattern from ** once again.

Repeat the pattern from *to* across the row (16 more times). When you come to the end, work a SK, skip the following 2 scs and work a dc in the last sc. Turn your work.

ROW 5

Ch 1 and work a sc in the first stitch.

Work 2 SKs and skip a SK as well as the next sc. Work a sc in the top of the next SK. Repeat the pattern from across the row, *i.e.* 34 more times. Turn your work.

ROW 6

Ch 1 and work a sc in the first stitch. Work 2 HSKs, and then 1 SK. Continue by working a sc in the top of the first SK.

Work 2 SKs and skip a SK. Work a sc in the top of the following SK. Repeat the pattern from across the row, i.e. 33 more times.

Work 1 SK and 1 drt in the last stitch. Turn your work.

ROW 7

Repeat the same as in ROW 5.

ROW 8

Repeat the same as in ROW 6.

ROW 9

Ch 1 and work a sc in the first sc.

Work a SK. Then, go to the top of the last SK and work the following sequence: ch 5, *yo and pull up a loop. Yo again and pull through 2 loops on the hook. Repeat the pattern from ** 3 more times. This makes a cluster. Then, ch 5 and sl st.

Work another SK, skip the next SK and the following sc. In the top of the following SK, work a sc.

Repeat the whole pattern from * to finish the row.

Chapter 4 – Spider Wrap

Yarn: 6-8 balls

Special instructions:

BASIC REPEAT (BR): skip the next 2 dcs and work 3 dcs in the next dc.

BASIC REPEAT 2 (BR2): 3 dcs in the next space between 3-dc groups

Begin by chaining 73.

ROW 1

Starting from the RS, go into the 4th chain from the hook and work a dc. Work a dc in each chain across the row.

ROW 2

Ch 3 and skip a dc. In the next dc, work 3 dcs. Work the BR 3 times.

Ch 11, skip 5 dcs and work 3 dcs in the next dcs. Then, work the BR 5 times. Repeat the pattern from once again.

Ch 11 again and skip 5 dcs. Work 3 dcs in the next dc. Work the BR 3 times.

To finish the row, skip a dc and work a dc in the last one. Turn your work.

In this row, you should have 20 groups of 3 dcs + 3 ch-11 spaces.

ROW 3

Begin by chaining 3 and working a dc in the first dc from the previous row.

Now, work the BR 3 times.

Ch 6 and work a sc in the ch-11 space. Then, ch 6 and repeat the BR2 5 times. Repeat the pattern from *to* once again.

Ch 6 again and work a sc in the ch-11 space. Ch 6 once again and work the BR2

3 times. When you come to the last dc, work 2 dcs in the same stitch and turn your work.

ROW 4

Ch 3 and work 3 dcs in the space between the first groups of 3 dcs. Then, work the BR2 twice.

*Ch 6 and work a sc in the ch-6 space. Continue by working a sc in the next stitch. Again, work a sc in the next ch-6 space.

Ch 6 and work the BR2 4 times.

Repeat the pattern from * once again. Then, ch 6 and work a sc in the next ch-6 space. Continue with a sc in the next sc and a sc in the next ch-6 space.

Ch 6 and work the BR2 two times.

When you come to the last group of 3 dcs, work 3 dcs in the space following the dc group. Work a dc in the last stitch and turn your work.

ROW 5

Begin by chaining 3 and work a dc in the first dc. Work the BR two times.

*Ch 6 and work a sc in the ch-6 space. Work a sc in the following 3 scs. Then, you come again to the ch-6 space. Work a sc here.

Work the BR2 3 times.

Repeat the pattern from * once again.

Continue by repeating the pattern from * again but work the BR 2 times. When you come to the last dc, work 2 dcs in the same stitch and turn your work.

ROW 6

Ch 3 and go into the space between the first groups of 3 dcs. Work 3 dcs here. Then, work 3 dcs in the next space between the group of dcs as well.

*Ch 6 and go into the ch-6 space. Work a sc here as well as in the following 5 scs. Then, work a sc in the next ch-6 space and ch 6. Work the BR2 two times.

Repeat the pattern once again. Continue by working the pattern from * but this time work the BR only once.

When you come to the last group of 3 dcs, work 3 dcs and a dc in the last dc. Turn your work.

ROW 7

Ch 3 and work a dc in the first stitch. Then, in the space between the next groups of 3 dcs, work 3 dcs.

*Ch 6 and work a sc in the ch-6 space. In the following 7 sc, work a sc, plus a sc in the ch-6 space. Ch 6 and go into the space between the groups of 3 dcs. Work

3 dcs here.

Repeat the pattern from * two more times.

When you come to the last dc in the row, work 2 dcs here and turn your work.

ROW 8

Begin the row by chaining 3 and working 3 dcs in the space between dc groups. Go into the ch-6 space and work 3 dcs here.

*Ch 6, skip a sc and work a sc in the following 7 scs. Ch 6 again and work 3 dcs in the following 2 6-ch spaces.

Repeat the pattern from * once again.

Begin repeating the pattern again, but this time you will work 3dcs only in one ch-6 space.

End the row by working 3 dcs in the space after the last group of 3 dcs in the row. Work a dc in the last stitch and turn your work.

ROW 9

Ch 3 and work a dc in the first stitch. Then, go into the space between the groups of 3 dcs and work 3 dcs. Go into the ch-6 space and work 3 dcs here.

*Ch 6, skip a sc and work a sc in the following 5 scs. Ch 6 and work 3 dcs in each ch-6 space and between the groups of 3 dcs. Repeat the pattern across the row.

To end the row, work 2 dcs in the last dc and turn your work.

ROW 10

Ch 3 and go into the space before the first group of 3 dcs. Work 3 dcs here and then do the same in the space between the following two dc groups as well as the ch-6 space.

Ch 6, skip a sc and work a sc in the following3. Ch 6 and work a dc in the ch-6 space. Work the basic patterns 2 two times and make another dc group in the ch-6 space. Repeat the pattern from across the row just pay attention that you make a group of 3 dcs into each space between dc groups and ch-6 space.

To end the row, work 3 dcs in the space after the final dc group. Work a dc in the last stitch and turn your work.

ROW 11

Ch 3 and work a dc in the first stitch. Repeat the BR2 two times and make a group of 3 dcs in the next ch-6 space.

*Ch 6, skip a sc and work a sc in the next one. Ch 6 again and make a group of 3 dcs in the ch-6 space.

Repeat the BR2 3 times. Then, work 3 dcs in the ch-6 space.

Repeat the pattern from * once again. Then, start repeating the pattern but you will work the BR2 two times instead of three.

To end the row, work 2 dcs in the last dc. Turn your work.

ROW 12

Ch 3 and go into the space before the first group of 3 dcs. Make 3 dcs here. Then, repeat the BR2 two times. Make 3 dcs in the ch-6 space.

Ch 11 and go into the ch-6 space. Work the BR2 4 times. Then, make 3 dcs in the ch-6 space. Repeat the pattern from one again.

Start repeating the pattern from * but this time you will have to repeat the BR that is within this repeat twice not 4 times.

In the last group of dc work 3 dcs and to end the row, work a dc in the last dc. Turn your work.

ROWS 13-112

Repeat Rows 3–12 ten times.

ROWS 113–121

Repeat Rows 3–11.

ROW 122

Begin by chaining 3 and making a group of 3 dcs before the first group of dcs. Repeat the BR2 two times. Work 3 dcs in the ch-6 space.

*Ch 5 and make a group of 3 dcs in the ch-6 space. Repeat the BR2 4 times. Then, create 3 dcs in the ch-6 space.

Repeat the pattern from *once again*. *After that, start working from the repeat* but make sure that you repeat the BR2 only twice.

End the row with a group of 3 dcs and a dc in the last stitch. Turn your work.

ROW 123

Ch 3 and work a dc in each of the following 12 dcs. Then, *work 4dcs in the ch-5 space and continue working a dc in each of the following 18 dcs from the previous rows.

Repeat the pattern from * once again. Continue following the pattern from * but you will have 12 instead of 18 dcs. When you come to the last dc, work a dc.

Fasten off. If you wish, you can add a border.

Chapter 5 – Love Knot Wrap/Pareo

Yarn – 1 – 2 balls

Special instructions:

Love knot: pull the loop on the hook to make it bigger. Make it ½-inch long. Yo and pull through the loop. Go into the chain that the big loop makes, yo and pull through the chain. Now you will have 2 loops on the hook. Yo and pull through both stitches. This will make a knot that secures the long loop.

ROW 1

Ch 1 and work 4 love knots. To connect them into a square, work a dc into the first ch. Turn your work.

ROW 2

Make 3 love knots. Then, go to the 3rd love know from the previous row and work a dc here. Then, work 3 more love knots and work a dc in the second love knot from the previous row. This will create 2 squares.

Turn your work. Make a love knot and connect it to the second love knot from the previous row with a dc. This is how you move to the next row.

ROW 3

Work 3 love knots and a dc in the top of the last square from Row 2. Then, make 2 more love knots and work a dc to connect it to the top of the next square.

To end the row, make 3 more love knots and connect it with a dc to the first love knot from the previous row. Turn your work.

In this row, you should have 3 squares.

ROW 4, *etc.*

Continue working love knots and creating squares until you get the desired size. You will have to work 3 love knots in the sides and 2 love knots across the row.

Chapter 6 – Butterfly Pareo

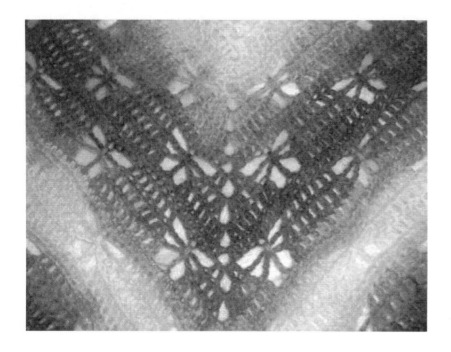

Yarn: 1 ball

Begin by chaining 6. Work a sl st to join the chains into a ring.

ROW 1

Ch 3 and turn. This will count as the first dc in this row. Work 5 dcs in the ring so that you now have 6 dcs in total.

ROW 2

Ch 3 and turn. In the first dc from the previous row, work 2 dcs. In the next one, work 3 dcs. Mark the second stitch to know where to work a treble stitch.

In the next one, work 3 dcs and then ch 2. Here you come to the center of the pareo.

Work 3 dcs in the next two stitches. Mark the second stitch from the second group of 3. To end the row, work 3 dcs in the 3rd turning chain of the previous row.

ROW 3

Ch 3 and turn your work. Go into the same first stitch and work 2 dcs. Then, ch 7 and skip the next 7 stitches.

Now you will come to the ch-2 space. Work a dc in the last dc before this space. Then, work 2 dcs and ch 2 and you come to the center point.

Work 2 dcs in the ch-2 space and 1 dc in the next dc. Again, ch 7 and skip the next 7 stitches. When you come to the last stitch, work 3 dcs.

ROW 4

Begin by chaining 3 and turn your work. As in the previous row, work 2 dcs in the same stitch. Then, work a dc in each of the following 2 dcs.

Ch 7 and work a dc in each of the following 3 dcs. Work 2 dcs and ch 2 and you come to the center point.

Work 2 dcs in the ch-2 space and continue by working a dc in each of the following 3 dcs. Ch 7 again and work a dc in each of the following 2 dcs. End the row by working 3 dcs in the last dc.

ROW 5

Ch 3 and work a dc in the same stitch. Then, work a dc in each if the following 3 dcs. Continue by working 2 dcs in the next dc and then ch 2.

When you come to the stitch you marked in Row 2, work a treble. Ch 2 and work 2 dcs in the next stitch. In each of the next stitches work a dc. When you come to the last dc, work 3 dcs.

ROW 6

Ch 2 and turn your work. Work a hdc in the same stitch. Continue working a hdc in every stitch across the row until you come to the center ch-2 space. Work a hdc in this space and then ch 2. Work another hdc in the ch-2 space and a hdc in every stitch across the row. When you come to the last stitch, work 2 hdcs.

ROW 7

Ch 3 and turn your work. Work 2 dcs in the same stitch. Ch 7 and then skip 7 stitches. Mark the 4th stitch.

In each of the following 7 stitches, work 1 dc and then ch 7. Skip the following 7 stitches and mark the 4th one.

Work a dc in the last hdc and then 2 dcs and ch 2. Now you come to the center point. Work 2 dcs in the ch-2 space and a dc in the next stitch.

Ch 7 and skip the following 7 stitches. Mark the 4th one and work a dc in each of the following 7 stitches. Ch 7 again and skip the next group of 7 stitches.

When you come to the last turning chain, work 3 dcs.

ROW 8

Ch 3 and turn your work. Work 2 dcs in the same stitch. Continue by working 1 dc in each of the next 2 dcs.

Then, ch 7 and skip 7 stitches. Work a dc in each of the next 7 stitches. Ch 7 again and skip 7 stitches again.

Work a dc in each of the next 3 stitches and work 2 dcs and ch 2. You come to the center point now. Work 2 dcs in the ch-2 space and a dc in each of the next 3 dcs.

Ch 7 again and skip 7 stitches. Work a dc in the next 7 dcs, ch 7 again and skip 7 stitches.

Work a dc in each of the following 2 dcs. In the turning chain, work 3 dcs.

ROW 9

Ch 3 and turn your work. Work 2 dcs in the same first stitch. Then, in each of the following 3 stitches, work a dc. In the next one, work 2 dcs. Ch 2 and work a treble in the stitch you marked. Ch 2 again and work 2 dcs in each of the next dc. In the next 5 dcs, work a dc and then 2 dcs in the next one.

Ch 2 and work a treble again in the stitch you marked.

Ch 2 and work 2 dcs in the next dc and a dc in each of the following 4 stitches. Then, work 2 dcs and ch 2. Now you come to the center point. Work 2 dcs into the ch-2 space and a dc in each of the following 4 dcs. Then, work 2 dcs in the next stitch and ch 2. Work a tr in the marked stitched.

Ch 2 and work 2 dcs in the next stitch. In the following 5 stitches, work 1 dc and 2 dcs in the next dc. Ch 2 again and work a tr in the marked stitch.Ch 2 again and work 2 dcs in the next dc and 1 dc in the following 3 dcs. End the row by working 3 dcs in the turning chain.

ROW 10

Ch 2 and turn your work. Work a hdc in the same stitch. Work a hdc in every stitch across the row.

Then, work a hdc and ch when you come to the center space. Work a hdc in the ch-2 space and continue working a hdc in every stitch across the row. To end the row, work 2 hdcs in the last turning chain.

ROW 11, *etc.*

To get the desired length, repeat the rows 7-10.

Chapter 7 – Lacy Wrap

Yarn: 6 balls

Special instructions:

VSt – work a dc, ch 2 and work another dc in the same stitch

Crossed stitch – skip the next stitch, work a dc in the next two stitches. Go back, working over the stitches you just made and work a dc in the skipped stitch.

Begin by chaining 66.

ROW 1

Go into the 5th chain from the hook and word a dc. Work a dc in the next ch as well. Work a dc in the 4th stitch working over the two stitches you just made.

Ch 1, skip one stitch and work a crossed stitch. Repeat this once again.

Then, ch 6, skip 6 stitches and *work a crossed stitch, ch 1 and skip 1. Then, work a crossed stitch once again, ch 1 and skip 1. Work another crossed stitch.* Ch 6 and skip 6 stitches. Repeat the pattern from *once again. Then, repeat the pattern from* to * once. To end the row, work a dc in the last stitch.

ROW 3

Ch 3 and turn your work.

*Work a crossed stitch and then ch 1 and skip 1 stitch. Work another crossed stitch, ch 1 and skip 1.

Work another crossed stitch, *ch 6 and skip 6 stitches. Repeat this pattern 2 more times. Then repeat the pattern from* to * once again. To end the row, work a dc in the last stitch.

ROW 3, *etc.*

All of the following rows are the same as Row 2. Repeat until you get the desired length.

EGDE

ROW 1

Start working on the long edge. With the RS facing, join in corner. Ch 5 and work a dc in the same stitch. This will count as a dc and ch 2.

*Evenly work dcs across the row until you reach the next corner. Here, work a dc, ch 2 and worn another dc.

Then, work dcs evenly until you come to the next corner.

In the corner, work a dc, ch 2 and work another dc. Repeat the pattern from once again. To end this row, join with a sl st to the 3rd stitch of the beginning chain, and then sl st to the center of the corner.

ROW 2

In the corner ch-2 space, work the following pattern: ch 3, dc, and then ch 3 again and 2 dcs. Then, skip 2.

Work a VSt in the next stitch and skip 2. Repeat this pattern until you are left with 2 stitches. Then, in the corner, work 2 dcs, ch 3 and 2dcs.

Repeat the pattern from *to* two more times. To end, work a VSt in the next stitch and skip 2 stitches. Sl st to the top of the beginning ch 3 and then sl st to the center of the corner.

ROW 3

In the corner ch-2 space, work the following group: ch 3, dc, ch 3, 2 dcs, and ch 1.

Work a VSt in the next VSt from the previous row. Repeat this until you come to the next corner. Then, in the corner work the same as in the corner from the beginning.

Repeat the pattern from *to* two more times. To end the row, work a VSt in the next VSt from the previous row and then ch 1. End the row in the same manner as the previous one.

ROW 4

Ch 1 and repeat this sequence 4 times: work 5 scs in the corner ch-3 space. Then work a sc in each stitch and ch-2 space to the next corner. End by joining with a sl st.

ROW 5

Ch 1 and work a sc in each stitch across the row but work only in the back loops.

Chapter 8 – Boho Pareo

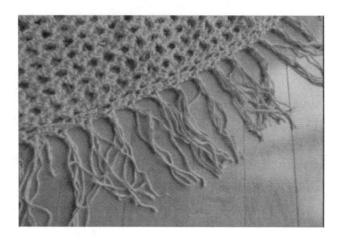

Special instructions:

Shell = 1 dc, 1 sc, 1 dc

ROW 1

Work a shell and then ch 2. Go into the 2nd chain of the beginning chain and work a dc.

Ch 4 and turn your work.

ROW 2

Work a shell in the ch-2 space from the previous row. Ch 2 and work another shell in the same space.

Ch 2 once again. Go into the 2nd chain of the beginning chain and work a dc.

ROW 3, *etc.*

The following rows are the same as Row 2. Repeat the row to get the desired length. Remember to begin your rows by chaining 4. When you come to ch-2 spaces, always work shells and ch 2 between shells. Don't forget to finish the rows with a dc.

Chapter 9 – Stripes & Squares Pareo

Yarn: 1 ball

To begin, ch 5 and join with a sl st to form a ring.

ROW 1

Ch 4 and work 4 trs. Then, ch 3 and work 5 trs in the ring. In this row, you should have 2 groups of 5 trs with ch 3 in between.

ROW 2

Ch 4 and turn your work.

Work 2 trc in the first stitch. This creates an increase. Then, in each of the next 4 stitches, work a tr. When you come to the ch-3 space, work 2 trs and then ch 2 and work 2 more trs.

In the next 4 stitches, work 1 tr. To end the row, work 3 trs in the top of the beginning ch 4 from the previous row.

ROW 3

Ch 5 and turn your work.

Work a tr in the same stitch and then ch 1. Then, work another tr in the same stitch and ch 1. This makes an increase.

Skip the next stitch and work a tr in the next one. Ch 1 and repeat the pattern from across the row. When you come to the ch-3 space, work a tr and ch 1 in the last stitch before this space.

Then, go into the ch-3 space and work a tr, ch 1 and work another tr. Then, ch 3 and work a tr, ch 1 again, work a tr and ch 1.

Now, move to the first stitch after the ch-3 space and *work 1 tr and ch 1. Skip the next stitch and work a tr in the next one and ch 1. Repeat the pattern from* across the row.

To end the row, go to the top of the ch 4 and work the following sequence: 1 tr, ch 1, 1 tr, ch, and 1 tr.

ROW 3

Ch 3 and turn your work. Go into the same first stitch and work 2 dcs.

Then, work a dc in each space until you get to ch-3 space. Here, work 2 dcs, ch 3 and then work 2 more dcs.

Then, work a dc in the next stitch and continue by working dcs evenly across the row. End the row by working 3 dcs in the top of the ch 4.

ROW 5, *etc.*

To get the desired length, repeat the Rows 3 and 4.

Chapter 10 – Old-Fashioned Wrap/Pareo

Yarn: 2-4 balls

Begin by chaining 6.

ROW 1

Sl st in the 1st chain to form a ring. Ch 6 and work 5 trs in the ring. Ch 5 and then work 5 trs in the same ring. Ch 3 and work a tr in the ring.

To end the row, ch 6 and turn your work.

ROW 2

Work 5 trs in the ch-3 space. Ch 3 and work 5 trc in the ch-5 space. Ch 5 and make another group of 5 trs in the same space.

Ch 3 and work 5 trc in the ch-3 space. Ch 3 and work a tr in the same space.

ROW 3, *etc.*

Repeat the same pattern until you get the desired length.

Finally, add the fringes to your pareo.

Conclusion

And now you have amazing crochet patterns for this summer. They may look as simple square or triangle wraps and pareo, but some patterns are actually based on such combinations of stitches that in the end give you a beautiful piece to add to your summer outfits. The book gives you 10 great crochet summer patterns of wraps and pareo. You just have to grab your hooks and yarns, choose a pattern, and you are ready to go.

10 Projects Of Trendy Crochet Shawls

Introduction

Following the patterns form the book will surely leave you with beautifully designed summer shawls. However, to make sure that your patterns really open up and reveal their beauty, there's one more thing to be done.

Once you finish your project, you should make sure to do something called blocking. As you may infer from the name itself, the process serves to "block" the pattern, *i.e.* to gently stretch the yarn interwoven into the work to show up the pattern in its best.

There are two ways to do this, and they will work interchangeably for most types of yarn and projects.

For the first method, you will need to prepare pins and a large wooden board or a piece of cardboard. Then, submerge your work, in this case shawl, into cold water, and after a few minutes, squeeze it gently. Then, place the shawl on the board and pin the edges down. I guess that the hardest part is to wait for the shawl to dry.

If you are wondering about a quicker method, here is one.

Lay the shawl on a flat surface and cover it with a damp towel or cloth. Pay attention that the cloth is not wet too much because the point here is to "steam" the shawl.

Then, take you iron, set it on low or medium and press over the damp cloth. Make quick movements (don't keep the iron on the cloth for more than 2 seconds). Remember – you don't need to iron the shawl but to steam it. And in just a few minutes, your shawl will be ready to show it off.

There's one more thing to be mentioned here. To make sure that you follow the instructions correctly, take a look at the abbreviations used in the book.

Ch = chain

Sc = single crochet

Dc = double crochet

Tr = treble / triple crochet Hdc = half double crochet I hope you will enjoy your summer with these crochet projects that will certainly add a note of elegance to your outfits.

Happy crocheting!

Chapter 1 – Lover's Knot Shawl

ROW 1

To begin, create a slip knot. Then, create 2 chain stitches. Go into the first chain stitch, yarn over and pull through. You now have 2 loops on your hook. Yarn over and pull through 2 loops. This creates a single crochet knot that anchors lover's knots to one another.

*To create a lover's knot, lengthen the working loop a bit (depending on the size of the knot you want).Ch 1, insert the hook in between the yarn strands that create the chain. Yarn over and pull through, and you now have 2 loops on the hook. Yarn over again and pull through 2. This is another sc knot that secures the lover's knot.

Repeat from * two more times to create three lover's knots in total. Join the last one to the first knot with a sc.

This way, you created the starting ring of lover's knots.

ROW 2

To begin Row 2, *create 3 lover's knots following the same steps as in the first row. Join the last one to the first knot on the right. Repeat from* to join three knots to the second knot on the right.

Since you are now at the side of Row 2, you will have to go back to Row 2 and create 2 lover's knots at the side, which will actually count as the beginning of the next row.

The diagram below can help you get a clearer image of the pattern.

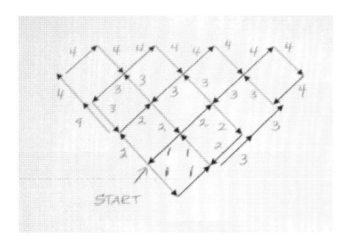

ROW 3

Start again with 3 lover's knots. Join to the closest knot to the left. Remember that in the previous row you worked towards the right? In this row, you will work towards the left, and don't forget to alternate the direction with every new row.

Then, you come to the middle part, so you will need only 2 lover's knots. Join them to the closets ring of knots following the same direction.

Again, create 3 lover's knots and join them to another ring of knots. And you come to the end of this row. You will again have to make two knots to go back to the row.

HOW TO CONTINUE?

Simply follow the same pattern over and over again. When you work in the middle, you will have to create only 2 lover's knots. On the other hand, when you work on the sides, you will need 3 lover's knots.

HOW TO FINISH?

When you reach the desired length of your shawl, work only 2 knots at the sides and 1 knot in the middle. If you wish, you can add fringes to the shawl.

Chapter 2 – Simple Summer Shawl

To begin, create the foundation chain.

ROW 1

Begin by skipping the first 2 chains and work a sc in the next chain. *Ch 3, skip 3 chains and in the next chain, work a dc, ch 1 and work another dc. This creates a V stitch. Skip 2 chains, work a sc in the next chain. Repeat the pattern from* across the row.

You should end this row with the equal number of scs, V stitches, and chain-3 spaces.

ROW 2

Begin with 3 chains and create a V stitch in the first stitch. Now, you come to a chain-3 space. *Sc here, ch 2 and create a V stitch in the next sc. Repeat the pattern from* across the row. When you reach the end, work a sc in the top of the turning chain.

HOW TO CONTINUE?

Just repeat Row 2 until you reach the desired length of your shawl.

HOW TO FINISH?

To begin the last row, ch 1 and work a sc in each stitch across the row.

To create the border, do not turn the work. You will work in the ends of rows across the side edge.

Begin by working *a sc, ch 1 and then work another sc around the turning chain of the next row. Ch 1 and skip the next sc row. Repeat the pattern from* all the way along the side edge of the last row and then ch 1.

Now, you will work along the opposite side of the first row. **Work a sc in the next chain and ch 1. Repeat the pattern from **across the edge. Create the border around the shawl and join with a slip stitch.

Chapter 3 – Infinity Shawl

Start with a slip knot and then ch 150. Join with a slip stitch to the first chain.

ROW 1

Ch 4 (that counts as a dc and ch 1). Skip the first chain and work a dc in the second chain.

Skip the next chain, ch 1 and dc into that second chain. Repeat the pattern from all the way around until you get to the beginning.

HOW TO CONTINUE?

This is the pattern that you will have to repeat for the whole scarf until you get the desired length.

HOW TO FINISH?

Work a dc into the chain space. Each dc is separated by ch 1. Keep doing it until the scarf is wide enough.

To finish it off, ch 1 and slip stitch into a chain space. Weave the tails and that's it.

Chapter 4 – Summer Berry Shawl

This shawl is made with multiples of 16 stitches plus ten.

ROW 1

To begin, make a sc into the second chain from the hook. *To start the first berry, ch 3, skip one chain, and sc in the next chain. And for each berry you begin, you will do this four times.

When you do this 3 more times, ch 5. Skip three chains and work a sc in the chain after that. Then, again ch 5, skip 3, and then work a sc in the chain after that.

Repeat from * across the row.

Now, to create another berry, repeat the steps from the beginning.

To finish the first row, ch 1 and dc in the last chain. It looks like a chain-3 loop.

ROW 2

Ch 1 and turn to begin Row 2. Work a sc in this chain space you created last in Row 1. *Ch 3 and sc in the next chain-3 loop. Repeat from* in every berry loop from the first row.

*Ch 5 and work a dc in the sc from the first row. Ch 5 and sc in the middle of chain-3 loop. Ch 3, sc in the next one, ch 3, sc in the next chain -3 loop and repeat this once again.

Repeat from * across the row. End the row with ch 1 and a sc.

ROW 3

Ch 1 and work a sc right into that chain 1 and double crochet space. Ch 3 and sc in the next one.

*Ch 5, and in the top of dc, work a V stitch (dc, ch 1, dc). Ch 5, sc in the top of the first berry from the previous row. Ch 3, sc in the chain-3 space, ch 3 and work another sc.

Repeat from * across the row. To finish the row, ch 1 and dc in the last stitch.

ROW 4

Work a sc in the first loop. Ch 3, sc in the next one, and you finished the first berry.

Ch 5 and work 5 dc in the chain-1 space of the V stitch. These 5 dcs are separated with chain 1.

Ch 5, and you are back to the middle berry. Work a sc in the first loop, ch 3, sc in the second loop and ch 5 again, and you are back to the V stitch. In the same space, create 5 dcs with chain 1 in between each.

Ch 5 and sc in the first loop (again in the middle of the berry). Finish the row with a dc.

ROW 5

Begin with a sc in the chain space.

Ch 5, and you will come to the group of 5 dcs. Sc in the first one, *ch 3, skip the chain-1 space, and sc in the next dc. Repeat from* until you come to the 4 starting berry loops.

Ch 5 and dc into a chain-3 space. Ch 5 and you come to the next set of 5 dcs. Here you will start the next berry (sc, skip chain-1 space, sc in the next dc).

Ch 5, and work a sc in the top of the chain-3 space of the last berry to finish the row.

ROW 6

Work a sc in the first chain-3 space. Ch 3 and sc in the next chain-3 loop. Repeat this 2 more times.

Ch 5 and dc into the top of the stitch in the middle. Ch 5, and then you come to the next chain-3 loop. Repeat the same steps as at the beginning of the row.

To finish the row, ch 1 and dc in the last chain-3 loop.

ROW 7

Work a sc in the chain space. *Ch 3 and sc in the next chain-3 loop. Repeat from* once again.

Ch 5 and work a V stitch into the top of the dc from the previous row.

Ch 5 and you are back to chain-3 loop. Work a sc here and repeat the pattern from * across the row.

ROW 8

Ch 1 and work a sc in the loop. Ch 3, sc in the next loop, ch 5, and create 5 dcs in the V stitch space with chain 1 in between each. Ch 5 and repeat the pattern from the beginning.

HOW TO CONTINUE?

Alternate the row patterns to create additional rows and reach the desired length. Keep in mind that you will have one berry less in each row you make.

HOW TO FINISH?

To work the edging, you can do slip stitches all around the shawl or you can even add fringes.

Chapter 5 – Boho Shawl

For this shawl, you will need to work with two strands of yarn and hold them together.

Begin by chaining 8. Slip stitch in the first chain to join and form a loop. This is the loop that you will build the pattern on.

ROW 1

Ch 5 (this will count as the first treble and chain 1). Work 2 trs in the starting loop you created. They are separated by ch 1. To create a third tr, ch 3 and work another tr in the same starting loop. Make 2 more trs.

ROW 2

Ch 4 (this will count as the first treble in this row). Work 3 trs in the chain-1 space. In each tr and chain-1 space, work one tr. When you come to the center space, work 2 trs, ch 3, and 2 more trs in the chain-3 space. Continue working 1 tr in each chain-1 space until you come to the final chain-1 space. Here, work 2 trs in the next chain-1 space and 2 trs in the final tr.

ROW 3

Begin with ch 4 (this will count as the first treble).

Work 2 trs in the first tr from the previous row. Work 1 tr in each tr until you come to the center chain-3 space. Use a stitch marker to mark this space and keep track of where you are in the row. Here, work 2 trs, ch 3 and work 2 more trs in the chain-3 space.

Continue working 1 tr in each tr from the previous row. When you come to the final 2 trs, work 2 trs in both of the final trs.

ROW 4

Ch 5 (this will count as the first treble and chain 1). Work 1 tr in the first tr from the previous row. Ch 1, and this will begin the repeat for this row. Skip 1 tr and work 1 tr in the next tr. Then, ch 1. Repeat the pattern until you reach the center chain-3 space. Here, you should work 1 tr, ch 3 and again 1 tr. You work this in the center chain-3 space.

Ch 1 again and work a tr in the next tr space. Again, ch 1 and repeat the pattern. When you come to the end of the row, ch 1 and work 1 tr, ch 1 and 1 tr in the final treble-space. Turn your work.

HOW TO CONTINUE?

To get the length you want, just keep repeating the rows 2-4.

HOW TO FINISH?

You can add some fringes to the shawl. Cut strands that are about 14 inches long or even longer if you wish. To make one fringe, fold several strands of yarn in half and loop them to the shawl.

Chapter 6 – Dragonfly Shawl

It is recommended to use paint metallic yarn because it gives a nice shine to the scarf.

ROW 1

Begin with a slip knot. Ch 30, 40, *etc.* until you get the desired length. Make sure to chain in groups of ten. When you get the length you want, add two more chains to it.

Insert the hook into the sixth chain from the hook. Yarn over and do a sc. *Ch7, skip 6 chains, and then go into the seventh one. Work a sc here. Ch 3, skip 2, and go into the third chain. Repeat from* till you come to the final stitch. Ch 1 and hdc into the final space.

ROW 2

From this round, you will begin your repeat pattern.

Ch 1, sc into the top of the hdc from the previous row. In this big gap, you will work 3 groups of 3 dc. So, dc into the gap 3 times and ch 1.

So, whenever you make a group of three, ch 1 to separate them. Repeat until you create 3 groups of 3.

Now, you come to a small gap space. Work a sc into this space. And then again do 3 groups of 3 dcs. Repeat that all the way across the row.

When you come to the end, go into the final chain-space to keep the work even.

ROW 3

Ch 9. Find the middle group of 3 dcs and sc into each of these three.

Ch 4 and go to the sc that you made in the small gap from the previous row. So, yarn over twice, go into that sc and do a tr.

Ch 4, go to the middle group of three and sc into each of the three. Ch 4, and repeat everything.

When you come to the end, tr into the final stitch.

ROW 4

Ch 1, sc into the top of the tr. Now ch 4. Find the middle of the three scs and work 2 dcs. Ch 4, sc into the top of the tr.

*Ch 3, and go into the same chain – so slip your hook in behind the stitches of the sc and slip stitch everything through. It will create a sort of a bump. Sc back into that same space.

Ch 4, work 2 dcs into the middle one of the three and ch 4. Sc into the top of the tr. Repeat from * across the row.

This creates a sort of a dragonfly shape.

When you come to the end, go into the fifth chain from the hook and work a sc.

ROW 5

Ch 7 and sc into the gap. *Ch 3, skip over the dcs and sc into the chain space on the other side of these dcs. Ch 7, skip over the dragonfly and sc on the other side.

Repeat the pattern from * until you reach the end of the row. Ch 4, dc into the sc from the previous row to keep it in balance.

ROW 6

Ch 3 and dc into this gap space. Ch 1 and dc three more times. This creates a half arch. Then, sc into the small gap spaces. Now you come to the big gap space. Make 3 groups of 3 dcs. Repeat this sequence across the row.

When you come to the end, you will have to do another half of the arch. So, do one group of 3 dcs. Ch 1 and work 1 dc but go into the third chain up to keep it even.

ROW 7

Ch 1 and dc into the first 2 dcs at the beginning.

Ch 4, go into the sc between the arches and do a tr. Then ch 4, go into the middle of the dc group and repeat the same from the beginning of the row.

ROW 8

Ch 3 and do a dc into the same stitch.

Ch 4 and work a sc into the top of the tr.

Ch 3, go into the top and the side of the sc stitch, and sc into that same stitch.

Ch 4, work 2 dcs into the middle as you did in Row 4.

You may have noticed that the rows are almost identical. They differ only in the way you begin them.

To finish the row, ch 3, and work 2 dcs in the last stitch.

ROW 9

This is the final row before the repeat.

Ch 4 and work a sc into the first gap space. Ch 7, go to the other side of the dragon fly and work a sc. Then, chain 3, and continue the same pattern as in Row 1. To finish the line, ch 1 and do a hdc into the final stitch.

HOW TO CONTINUE?

Keep repeating the rows to reach the desired length. The next row, Row 10, is the same as Row 2.

Chapter 7 – Fortune Shawl

ROW 1

Begin with a slipstitch and ch 6. Go into the fourth chain from the hook and work a dc. Ch 1, skip the next chain and dc in the very last chain. So, this is the first block of the pattern.

ROW 2

Ch 6 and dc in the fourth chain from the hook. Chain 1, skip the next chain and dc into the next chain (which is the first of the six you made).

Remember that in the first row you skipped chain-3 space to work a dc? Now work a slip stitch into this chain-3 space and that anchors the block two of Row 2 down.

The second block of Row 2 is also to be worked in this chain-3 space. Begin with 3 chains again and then dc into that chain space, ch 1 and dc into that chain-3 space again.

HOW TO CONTINUE?

All the next rows are the same as the previous one. Keep in mind that the number of blocks is the same as the number of row. Keep in mind that every time you come to the chain-3 space, you slip stitch.

When you reach the length you desire, you will have to make an edge.

HOW TO FINISH?

To make a straight edge, ch 4, skip the chain closest to the hook, and work a sc in the next chain. *Ch 1, skip the next chain and work a dc in the chain after that. Make a slip stitch into the chain-3 space. Repeat from* across the row.

To create a decorative edge, do not turn your work. Instead, turn the work up so that the point where you started with the Row 1 is upside. So, you will work along the sides of the rows so that the Row 1 is the point of the shawl that will hang down.

ROW 1 of the decorative edge

Ch 1, and in the side of each block, including the last one, work 2 scs all the way down towards the point.

When you come to the point, work 2 scs there and 1 sc right at the point into the loop. You can use a stitch marker to make sure that you always know which one is the center point.

When you come to the end, work a sc into the loop at the edge to keep the edge straight.

ROW 2 of the decorative edge

Ch 2 and turn the work. Work a dc into the very first stitch. Ch 3 and dc into the same stitch.

Skip 2 stitches, work a dc, ch 2 and dc into the same stitch. Repeat from until you come to the middle point. Then, work 2 dcs, ch 2, and dc into the point stitch. Then, if you skipped one between the last two dc and the point, skip one again, and continue working the pattern.

ROW 3 of the decorative edge

Ch 2, work a dc into the last dc you made in the previous row. Towards the point, work 2 dcs into the chain-3 space. Ch 2 in between each of these. When you come to the middle point, work 5 dcs.

Ch 2 and continue the pattern all the way down. When you come to the end, make sure to finish off in the very last stitch to keep the edge straight.

ROW 4 of the decorative edge

Ch 1 and turn the work. Skip the last stitch you made and slip stitch into the next. Ch 3 and slip stitch in the next stitch. To get to the next group of dc, *ch 2, slip stitch in the first dc from the group, ch 3, and slip stitch in the second one. Repeat from* until you get to the middle point.

Ch 2, slip stitch in the first one, ch 3, slip stitch in the second one, and slip stitch right away in the third one. Ch 3 and slip stitch again in the same stitch to keep it centered. Slip stitch in the next one, ch 3 and slip stitch in the last one. Repeat till you reach the other end of the scarf.

Chapter 8 – Alpaca Shawl

When working on this shawl, keep in mind that this pattern is worked in multiples of 8 plus 4. So, chain as many chains as you need to reach the desired length.

ROW 1

Begin with yarn over and dc in the fifth chain from the hook. Work in the back part of the chain only. Ch 1, skip 2, and in the chain after that do a dc. Ch 3 and then dc in the same stitch (you will create a stitch that looks like a V stitch).

Then, skip 1 stitch and work a dc but leave 2 chains on the hook (so you basically do not finish that double crochet) and then skip 2 chains and work a dc so that you finish the second half of the first dc (when you have 3 loops on the hook, pull through all 3). And now you will have only one, *i.e.* working loop on the hook. Repeat this sequence across the row.

When you come to the end, you should have four chains left. Ch 1, skip 2, and in the last 2 chains work 2 dcs to create a V stitch.

ROW 2

This row will start the pattern repeat. Start with ch 3 (treat this as a dc) and ch 2 more (so you have 5 chains in total, so treat this as a dc + chain 2). Turn your work.

You will do a dc in the top of the first dc of that V stitch from the first row. Then, do 2 dcs into the chain-3 space. Work the next dc into the last dc in that group from Row 1.

Ch 2, and in the top of that decrease from Row 1, work 1 dc. Ch 2 and that is the repeat for this row.

When you come to the very end of the row, do a dc in the top of chain-3 space.

ROW 3

Ch 4 (this will act as a dc and ch 1). Dc right in the top of the dc you made at the end of the previous row. Ch 1 (here you come to a group of 4 dcs), insert the hook in the first leg of the first dc and pull through.

Now you have 2 loops on the hook. Yarn over, go into the second leg of the last dc, yarn over, pull through two, yarn over and pull through all three. This creates a decrease in the row.

After this decrease, ch 1, move on to a single dc sitting there and work one of wide Vs – ch 3, and dc into the top of that lone dc from the previous row. Then you come to a group of four again, so you do a decrease once again.

Repeat this sequence until you reach the end of the row. When you come to the end of the row, ch 1 and work a dc in the top of that chain-4 space.

ROW 4

Begin with 3 chains. Work a dc in the second dc of the V stitch from the previous row. Ch 2, you come to a decrease, so work 1 dc. Ch 2 and you come to a wide V. So, work a dc in the first one and 2 dcs in the chain space, and then do a dc in the second half of the wide V.

Ch 2 and you come again to a decrease, so work a dc on top of that. Repeat these steps across the row.

To end the row, ch 2, work a dc in the last regular dc from the previous row, and then work another dc in the third chain from the chain 4 from the previous row.

ROW 5

Ch 3 and work a dc not in the last dc but the next one from the previous row. Ch 1 and you come to a lone dc, so work a wide V here. Ch 1, and you come to a set of four dcs. Work a decrease here. Ch 1, and repeat the same steps across the row.

When you come to the end, work 2 dcs to create a V stitch.

HOW TO CONTINUE?

The basic repeat is Row 2, Row 3, Row 4, Row 5, Row 2, Row 3, Row 4, Row 5, *etc.*

HOW TO FINISH?

To create a border, work a row of dcs in each stitch.

Chapter 9 – Broomstick Lace Shawl

For this project, you will also need a size 50 knitting needle or you can use a wooden dowel instead.

ROW 1

To begin, make a slip knot and ch 30. This is for a small shawl of 10 inches. If you want a bigger shawl (say, 20 inches), ch 60.

Lengthen your loop and insert the knitting needle into this loop. Insert the crochet hook into the next chain, yarn over, draw a loop and gently place it on the knitting needle. Repeat this for all the remaining chains. You should end up with 30 or 60 loops on the knitting needle.

ROW 2

In this row, you will take off the loops in groups of 3. Insert the crochet hook under the first 3 loops on your knitting needle. Move the hook to the top of the needle and ch 1. Pull the loops off the needle. Make 3 scs in these 3 loops.

Repeat the same with the remaining loops.

ROW 3

Lengthen the working loop and insert the knitting needle. In this row, you will work only in the back loops. So, insert your hook into the back loop, yarn over and draw up a loop. Gently place this loop on the needle. Repeat the same across the row.

ROW 4

Now, when you end up either with 30 or 60 loops on the knitting needle, insert the hook under the first 3 loops, move the hook to the top side of the needle and ch 1 on top of these 3 loops. Pull off the loops off the needle and do 3 scs in the middle of the group of 3. Repeat the same across the row.

HOW TO CONTINUE?

Repeat this pattern until you reach the length you desire. This one has 90 rows. Always end on a row where you have completed single crochet.

HOW TO FINISH?

You can cut off the yarn and weave in the end or incorporate the end as a part of a fringe. To create a fringe, cut several strands (about 14 inches long) and fold them in half. Finally, loop them at the end of your shawl.

Chapter 10 – Flower Of Life Shawl

ROW 1

To begin, create a slip knot and then ch 4. Then, work a slip stitch to form a loop and connect it to the first chain.

Ch 15 and slip stitch into the middle of the ring. So, you will now have one ring attached to the starting ring. Do another set of 15 chains. Slip stitch into the middle of the ring again.

Repeat these steps until you get 5 large rings around the middle, starting ring.

ROW 2

To begin the next row, ch 1 and turn your work. Now, slip stitch up along one side of the first ring. When you come to the center of this first ring, ch 15 to create another ring. Slip stitch into the top of the loop stitch (the one up to which you slip stitched along the ring).

Ch 15 again to create another loop. Slip stitch to the same place where you slip stitched before. Now you have 2 big rings attached to the ring from the first row.

Now, ch 5 to help you get over to the next ring from the first row. Find the center loop of this ring, insert the hook and do a slip stitch into this top center loop. *Ch 15 again, and slip stitch in the same slip stitch as before. Repeat once again.

To get over to the next ring from the Row 1, ch 5. Find the center of the ring and slip stitch into it. *Ch 15, slip stitch into the same slip stitch as before. Repeat two more times.

Ch 5 to get over to the next loop. Slip stitch to the top of that loop. *Ch15 again, slip stitch into the same slip stitch. Repeat once again.

Ch 5 to get over to the last loop and slip stitch into the top of the last loop.

Ch 15 and slip stitch and repeat once again.

ROW 3

This row is almost identical to the previous one. The only difference is that now you will have to chain 7 to get over to the next loop.

HOW TO CONTINUE?

Repeat Row 3 until you get the desired length.

HOW TO FINISH?

If you wish, add fringes to your shawl.

Conclusion

And you have come to the end of this collection of summer crochet shawls. This set of crochet projects will surely keep you occupied with their simple stitches combined into delicate and elegant patterns. Besides the instructions on how to crochet these summer shawls that will give your outfits a note of elegance and femininity, the book also teaches you one essential process in crocheting. This is blocking. *i.e.* allowing your projects time to "open up" their patterns and show their beauty. Hope you enjoyed the summer crochet projects.

Crochet
10 Projects Of Sweet Crochet Rugs

Introduction

Crochet maybe used to be a favorite pastime of our grandmothers, but the truth is that it has recently become pretty popular. A growing number of both men and women discover the beauty of this craft. Some even turn their love for crochet hooks and yarn into their job and earn their income by selling their crochet projects.

In this book, you ' ll find rug patterns that give you freedom to be as imaginative with colors and materials as you like. So, who says that you should use only regular yarn? If you want your rugs to be sturdier, you can use ropes, old sheets,and T-shirts. Yes, you read that right. You can save some money by recycling old stuff, and plus, you ' ll turn them into something new and useful.

In case you have never crocheted with tarn (T-shirt yarn), here ' s how to make it.

When choosing the material for your projects, make sure that T-shirts are mostly made of cotton and that there is no or is very little print on them. Also, try to choose fabric that is fairly consistent in weight. Otherwise, you may end up with a rug that has stitches of different size, which may affect the overall quality of the rug.

Once you choose an appropriate fabric, you can go on and create your yarn. When cutting your T-shirts or any other material to form yarn, you should consider the width of strips. Obviously, the thicker strips will give you thicker yarn. You should also think about the project itself and choose the width accordingly. I would recommend the width of 1-2 inches.

When cutting T-shirts, you should go around so that you cut a continuous strip. In case it is easier for you to cut straight, you can later on sew the strands together and turn them into one long strip. Also, make sure to cut only up to the armpit. You should also remove the hem before cutting because it doesn't curl and won't form yarn.

Once you finish cutting, stretch the strip(s) and allow them to curl on their own. This way, the strip(s) will form the yarn you can use for crocheting rugs. Finally, ball up your yarn, and you are ready to start crocheting.

If you have old sheets, you can follow the same procedure. And when it comes to ropes, it is pretty simple – use them as you would use any regular yarn.

So, it's pretty much everything you need to know before you grab your crochet hook and start creating these amazing rugs. Surround yourself with colorful yarns, pick a pattern and you are ready to go. Enjoy your crocheting!

Chapter 1 – Cozy Rag Rug

For this rug, you can either use super bulky yarn or some recycled material, such as strands of old sheet or T-shirts. Choose the size of a crochet hook depending on the material you decide to use as yarn.

How to begin?

Start by making a slip knot but make sure that it is very loose. Yarn over and pull up a loop. Reach through again and pull up another loop.

Round 1

Now, do a single crochet into the slip knot. Pull up only through the slip knot so that you now have two loops on your hook. Reach through and pull through both loops. That's one single crochet, and you will repeat this through the whole rug.

Reach back into the initial single crochet, pull up again so that you have two loops on your hook. Grab the yarn again, pull up, and that's the second single crochet.

Work six single crochets all into the first slip knot. Now, take the tail and pull it gently to tighten the hole in the middle.

Use a stitch marker and place it onto the final stitch of every round to keep track.

So, now you have six single crochets, and you will be working only in the back loop of them. This way, the front loop will form a spiral.

Round 2

Insert your hook into the back loop of the first single crochet and work another single crochet. Then, work another single crochet into that first stitch.

Repeat this sequence in the back loop of every stitch around.

In this round, you should have 12 single crochets. Once you finish this round, mark the final single crochet with your stitch marker and move on to the next round.

Round 3

Now, you will do two single crochets in the first one and then one single crochet in the next stitch. Remember to work only in the back loop.

Continue that pattern all the way around, and you should end up with 18 stitches. Mark the final stitch and go on.

Round 4

In this round, you should follow this sequence: two single crochets in the same stitch, one single crochet in each of the next two stitches and continue this pattern across the row.

In this round, you will end up with 24 stitches.

Round 5

This round has the following sequence: two single crochets in the first stitch, and one single crochet in each of the next three stitches.

Round 6

For Round 6, follow this pattern: two single crochets in the first stitch and one single crochet in the next four stitches.

Rounds 7, 8, 9, *etc.*

If you want your rug to be bigger, just keep increasing or adding six stitches in each round.

How to finish off?

To finish off, you should work two slip stitches and pull the rope up.

To hide the end, push the tail through the side of the next loop and poke it back down from the one where it came. That creates a fake loop and looks like it ends seamlessly with the edge.

Chapter 2 – Rainbow Rug

For this rug, you can use a regular yarn and a hook of a matching size. Since the rug should be in the colors of a rainbow, choose green, yellow, red, orange, blue, and purple yarns for this project.

Feel free to arrange the colors as you would like your rug to look like. The only thing to remember is that when you change colors, you should join them with a slip stitch at the chain-one space. When you don't change colors, just work a simple slip stitch.

How to begin?

Start with the yellow yarn. Make a magic ring or chain four and join with a slip stitch.

Round 1

Chain three and work two double crochets into the ring. Chain one and do three more double crochets into the middle. You will have five groups of double crochets, *i.e.* five groups of shells.

Join on the top of chain-three and then slip stitch to join.

Round 2

You can change color here and switch to orange. Join in, chain three and work two double crochets in the same space.

Chain one and work three double crochets in the same space. This is one shell.

Now, you will need to increase. So, go into the next chain-one space, work three double crochets and then chain one. To finish with this increase space, work three double crochets into the same space.

In this round, you will do increase in every chain-one space.

Now join at the top of chain-three space and do a slip stitch.

Round 3

If you do not change colors, slip stitch across the row at the top of stitches as well as the chain-one spaces.

To begin this round, chain three and work two double crochets in the same space.

Move on to the next space and work three double crochets. Chain one and then do three double crochets again in the same space.

The pattern you should repeat in this round is the following one: shell (three double crochets in the same space) and increase (six double crochets in the next space).

Join at the top of the chain-three space and work a slip stitch.

Round 4

You can change color in this round. Cut off the yarn and join the new yarn in the next space.

Begin by chaining three. Work two double crochets in the same space. In the next space, you will work three double crochets, chain one and again three double crochets (this is an increase). Continue with a shell and then again increase. Work this pattern across the row.

Finish by joining at the top of the chain-three space with a slip stitch.

Round 5

As with the previous rounds, chain three and double crochet in the same space two times (this is our beginning shell). Continue with three double crochets in the next spot.

And now comes the increase – six double crochets in the same spot.

So, the pattern to repeat in this round is shell – shell – increase.

To finish this round, join at the top of the chain-three space as with all the other rounds.

Round 6

You will begin this round with the increase. So, chain three and double crochet five times in the same spot. Then, do a shell in each of the next three spaces. Continue with the increase and go on alternating between the increase and three shells.

Round 7

Start this round with the beginning shell – chain three and two double crochets. This is a plain round, which means there is no increase. So, you will work a shell in every space.

Round 8

Make a beginning shell followed by an increase in the next space. Then, do a shell in each of the following four spaces. The next space will be an increase and that makes the pattern for this round – increase – four shells – increase – four shells.

Round 9

After the beginning shell, do a shell in the next four spaces so that you have five shells in total. Then, do an increase. Repeat this pattern across the row.

Round 10

This is the same round as Round 7. So, shell in every space.

Now is the right time to check if your rug is lying flat. If you notice that it has started to curl up, switch to a larger hook.

Round 11

For this round, you will do a beginning shell and continue doing shells in the next six spaces. Now do an increase and repeat the pattern all the way around.

Round 12

As all the other rounds, this one also starts with a beginning shell. For the next four spaces, you will also have to do a shell in each and then continue with an increase. The pattern for this round ends with a shell in the next seven spaces.

So, after an increase, work a shell into the next seven spaces and repeat this sequence.

Round 13

This one is easy. It's the same as Round 7 – shell in every space.

Check the rug again. If it begins to curl up, skip Round 14.

Round 14

Again, it's the same as Round 7.

Round 15

Chain three and do a shell in four spaces. Then, you'll have to do an increase in the next and continue with a shell in the next eight spaces. Increase again and repeat the pattern – shell in eight spaces – increase.

Round 16

This is also an increase round. So, the pattern is: shell in nine spaces – increase – shell in nine spaces.

Round 17

This round is the same as Round 7 – a shell in every space.

Check if the rug is lying flat. If it begins to curl up, go straight to the increase round, *i.e.* Round 19.

Round 18

Repeat Round 7 again.

Round 19

Start with a beginning shell and then do a shell in the next 7 spaces so that you have 8 shells in total. The next space will be an increase.

Go on and do a shell in each of the next ten spaces. Increase again and repeat – 10 shells – increase.

How to finish?

Round 20

Begin by chaining five. Then, yarn over twice and go into the stitch. Pull up, yarn over and pull through two. Yarn over, pull through two loops on your hook, yarn over and pull through the remaining two.

So, you will work in the three stitches of a shell. In the first one, you will do a double crochet. The second one will be a half double crochet, and the next one is a single crochet. Once you do these, you will go backward – do a single stitch, half double crochet, and a double crochet.

Now, you have come to the beginning. *Yarn over twice, go into a stitch, and pull up a loop by pulling through two loops at a time (remember to yarn over in between). Chain one and repeat from* once again into the same spot.

Repeat this whole sequence all the way around to finish this round. To join the ends, make sure to join into the top of the fourth chain from the chain-five and then do a slip stitch.

Round 21

If you wish, you can join a new color.

Chain one and work two single crochets. Then, chain three and slip stitch into the top loop *i.e.* front loop of the single crochet there and go into the side loop as well.

Work two single crochets into the same space.

Do three single crochets across and decrease over the next two stitches. So, go into the loop and pull up. Go into the next loop again and pull up and pull through.

*Do a single crochet in the next three stitches and two single crochets in the chain space. Once again, chain three and slip stitch into the top loop *i.e.* front loop of the single crochet there and go into the side loop as well.

Repeat from * across the whole row. Join the ends and that's it.

Chapter 3 – Shaggy Rug

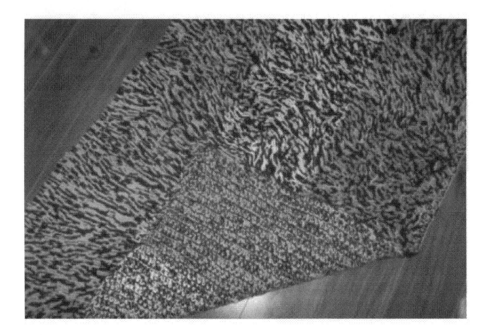

For this rug, you can use regular yarn, and if you wish, you may work with two strands held together.

How to begin?

Begin by creating half double crochet foundation stitches. Or, if you prefer, you can chain as many stitches as you like and then half double crochet in the third stitch from your hook. And then do a half double crochet in each chain.

Round 1

Chain one and turn your work. Yarn over and go into the first stitch. Then, create a loop of yarn with your finger. Just wrap the yarn around your finger, and then place the hook on top of the bit of yarn that is the closest to your project. Go behind it with the hook and underneath so that you grab the bit of yarn that is the farthest from your project and is around your finger.

When you grab that bit of yarn, bend your finger and that will pull this bit of yarn closer to your project. The point is to bring closer that bit of yarn that you hooked through the stitch so that you have three loops on the hook. Now, you can let your finger off the loop. Yarn over and pull through all three and that completes the half double crochet loop stitch. Repeat this for each stitch across.

You don't need to worry if you don't make loops of equal size.

Round 2

Chain one and do one half double crochet in each stitch across.

Round 3

This is the same row as in Round 1. So, do another row of loop stitches.

The key to the pattern is to alternate between the rows of half double crochets and loop rows.

How to finish?

To finish with your rug, do a simple, half double crochet row.

The last thing to do is to clip the loops so that they become single strands. If they are not of equal length, you can trim them as you desire.

Chapter 4 – Fake Carpet Rug

To make this rug, you can either work in many small rectangles that you will later join together or you can crochet one big rug.

How to begin?

Create a slip knot and chain as many stitches as you like to match the size you need.

Round 1

The first row is a simple, single crochet row.

At the end of the row, chain five stitches and turn your work.

Round 2

Yarn over three times and then crochet into the front loop only. Pull through two loops only, and then pull through the remaining two. Do the same across the row. Of course, you can do more yarn overs or less depending on how you want your rug to look like. If you want it to be fluffier, just yarn over more than two times.

Now, fold the stitches and join them with single stitches but work through the back loop of the first row.

Round 3

Then, chain one, turn your work, and single crochet across the row.

Round 4

This round is the same as Round 2.

Fold your stitches and join them with single crochets but now go through the front loop.

You can crochet as many rows as you want. However, remember to alternate between a single crochet row and the one with loops. Also, it is important to alternate between front and back loops as well.

Chapter 5 – Old-Fashioned Granny Rug

How to begin?

Start with a magic ring.

Round 1

Chain three, make one double crochet and chain one. Repeat this 11 times and close with a slip stitch.

Round 2

Chain three, work a double crochet in the next stitch and chain one. *Skip one stitch and in the next one do two double crochets and then chain one. Repeat from* across the row and close with a slip stitch and one more slip stitch in the next stitch.

Round 3

Chain three and in the next stitch do two double crochets and then chain one. Skip two stitches and in the next one do three double crochets and chain one. Repeat this all the way around. Close with a slip stitch and one more slip stitch in each of the next two stitches.

Round 4

Chain three and do a double crochet in the next stitch. Chain one and then do two double crochets and chain one again.

Skip three stitches and in the next one do two double crochets. Chain one, do two double crochets and chain one again. Repeat this sequence all the way around.

Close with a slip stitch and one more slip stitch in the next stitch.

Round 5

Chain three and in the next stitch do one double crochet and then chain one. Skip two stitches and in the next one do two double crochets and chain one. Repeat this pattern across the row.

Close with a slip stitch and one more slip stitch in the next stitch.

Round 6

This round is the same as Round 3.

Round 7

Chain three and in the next stitch do two double crochets. Chain one and skip three stitches.

In the next one, do three double crochets and chain one. Repeat this across the whole row.

Close with a slip stitch and one more slip stitch in each of the next two stitches.

Round 8

Change color and repeat the same steps as in Round 4.

Round 9

This round is the same as Round 5.

Round 10

Chain three and in the next stitch do a double crochet and then chain one. Skip two stitches and in the next one do two double crochets and chain one. Repeat this across the whole row.

Close with a slip stitch and another slip stitch in the next stitch.

Round 11

This round is the same as Round 6.

Round 12

This round is the same as Round 7, but it ends with one slip stitch.

How to finish?

Round 13

Chain five. Skip three stitches and in the next one do one slip stitch. Repeat this across the row. Only the last one will be different. Chain two, skip three and in the next one do a slip stitch and a double crochet.

Round 14

Chain three and in the same starting stitch do two double crochets. In each of the next two stitches do one double crochet. In the third chain of the next mountain of stitches, do a slip stitch.

In the first and the second chain of the next mountain of stitches do a double crochet.

In the third chain, do four double crochets.

In the fourth and fifth chain do a double crochet.

In the third chain of the next mountain of stitches make a slip stitch.

Repeat the same all along the rug until you get to the starting point of this round. Here, in the first and second chain of the last mountain of stitches, make a double crochet. And in the third chain of the starting point, do one double crochet.

Close with a slip stitch.

Chapter 6 – Cotton Rope Rug

How to begin?

Instead of regular yarn, you can use rope for this rug.

Start with a magic circle. Make two chain stitches and 11 double crochets. Close with a slip stitch.

Round 1

Start with three chain stitches and one double crochet. Do treble crochet in all the stitches. Close the row with a slip stitch. Remember that the last stitch will be a double crochet that will join the three chains from the beginning.

Round 2

Start with three chain stitches, *1 double crochet, 1 treble crochet. Repeat this sequence and close with a slip stitch. Remember that the last stitch will always be a double crochet that will join the three chains from the beginning.

Each row from now on increases one stitch at the sequence.

Round 3

Chain three, and do three double crochets in the next three stitches. Then, do two double crochets in the same stitch and repeat this pattern across the row.

Round 4

Change color and do an increase row. You can arrange colors as you like.

How to finish?

Once your rug is big enough, cast off that that's it.

Chapter 7 – Spring Rug

For this simple rug, you will need to work with super bulky yarn.

How to begin?

Begin by chaining 33 stitches. If you want to make a wider rug, add more stitches.

Round 1

The first round is simple. Just slip stitch in every stitch and turn your work.

Round 2

Chain one and slip stitch in the back loop of the next stitch. Repeat in each stitch across the row.

Turn your work.

The key is to work only in the back loops.

All the rounds to follow are exactly the same as Round 2. You will just need to change color.

Chapter 8 – Simple Rectangle Rug

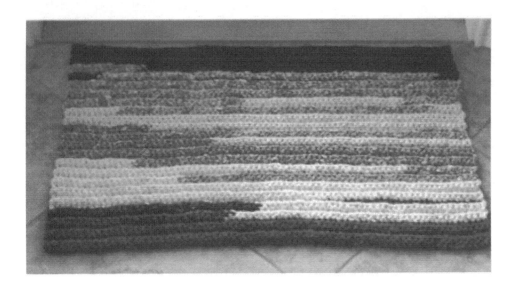

This is one of those rugs where you can recycle old T-shirts and make new, amazing stuff. So, instead of regular yarn, you should use strands made of old T-shirts. If not sure how to make them, go back to the Introduction.

How to begin?

Begin with a foundation chain and 76 stitches.

Round 1

Start in the second chain from the hook and single crochet across the whole row.

Round 2

Turn your work, chain one and single crochet in the back loop starting from the second loop from the hook. Repeat this pattern all the way across the row.

All the following rounds are the same as this one. You can repeat the rounds as many times as you wish. Of course, feel free to change colors and make your rug lively and colorful.

How to finish?

The last row is the same as Round 2, but you should make it a bit tighter so that the rug gets a neat edge.

To finish off, weave in the ends and that's it.

Chapter 9 – T-Shirt Granny Crochet Rug

How to begin?

Begin with a magic circle.

Round 1

The first round consists of six single crochets in the same space creating a circle and the base for the remaining rounds.

Round 2

To increase the row, work two single stitches in each stitch. So, you should end up with 12 stitches.

Round 3

Begin with one single stitch and then go on and work two single stitches in the next spot. Repeat this sequence so that you end the round with 18 stitches.

Round 4

In this round, you will do a single stitch in the first two stitches of the row. The next stitch will have two single stitches. Repeat this pattern across the row. This row should have 24 stitches.

Check if the rug is lying flat. If it has started to curl up, it means that you need more stitches in the round.

Round 5, 6, 7, *etc.*

For more rounds, keep working single crochet and adding six new stitches to each round.

Chapter 10 – Natural Stripes Rug

When crocheting this rug, you will have to work with two strands and hold them together. Also, use two colors to get a nice effect of a subtle color change.

How to begin?

Start by chaining 71 chains. Make sure that they are loosely chained. Use two strands of the same color.

Round 1

Go into the second chain from the hook. Pull up a loop and repeat the same in the next chain. Yarn over and draw through all three loops on the hook.

Now, you will begin with the repeat: go into the same chain and pull up a loop, go into the next chain, yarn over and pull through all three loops on the hook. Repeat this pattern across the row.

To finish the row, do a single stitch in the same chain as the last leg of the last stitch. You should end up with 70 stitches. Turn your work and move to Round 2.

Round 2

Chain one, go into the first stitch and pull up a loop. Repeat the same in the next stitch. Yarn over and pull through all three loops on your hook.

To start your repeat, go into the same stitch as the last leg of the last stitch and pull up a loop. Go with your hook into the next stitch, yarn over and then pull through all the three loops on the hook. Repeat this pattern across the row.

To finish this row, do a single stitch in the same stitch as the last leg of the last stitch. Also, at the end of the row, you should change to one strand of both colors.

In this row, you should have 70 stitches. Turn your work and move to Round 3.

Round 3 – 6

The rows that follow will be the same as Rounds 1 and 2. To achieve a nice color effect, you should just pay attention to change strands according to the instructions here.

Repeat Rounds 1 and 2 twice. Once you get to the last single stitch of Round 6, change to two strands of the other color (not the one you started with).

Round 7-10

Do the same as you did in Rounds 3-6, but now you will work with two strands of the same color.

Round 11-14

These rounds are the same as Rounds 3-6, but you will work with two strands of different color.

Round 15-18

The pattern is the same but this time, you will work with two strands of the color you started with.

Round 19-48

Both for the pattern and color change, repeat the rounds from 3 to 18 two times.

Round 49-52

These are the same rows as in Round 3-6.

Round 53-56

Do the same as in Round 7-10.

Round 57-60

These rounds are the same as Round 11-14.

Round 61-62

Follow the same pattern as in Rounds 3 and 4.

How to finish?

To create a tight edge around the rug, switch to a smaller hook. Work one round of single crochet in every stitch. At each corner, work three single crochets. Now, you just have to weave in the ends, and that's it.

If you want your rug to have fringes, you can cut about 7-inch lengths of the strands and knot them on both ends of the rug.

Conclusion

And you've come to the end of this amazing collection of crochet rug patterns. But before you even begin any project, you first have to acquire materials. Besides regular yarn, the rugs in this book can also be made with the yarn you can get from old sheets or T-shirts. The introductory part teaches you how to turn old fabric into yarn.

Then, the book gives you instructions on crocheting 10 lovely rugs for your home. It was a truly interesting exploration of color and pattern variations. You've got several new projects to keep your yarn and hook occupied and to furnish your home with these lovely rugs. Hope you enjoyed these projects.

Crochet Projects
25 Neat Crochet Projects
Of Hats And Scarves
That Will Warm And Comfort You

Introduction

If you have learned basic crochet patterns and you want to move forward to make something that you can wear in your everyday activities, this book is just perfect for you.

Crocheting is more than just an artwork. It involves putting the maker's love into every details made in the finished products. Therefore, besides to make crochet as a hobby, you can also make it as special gifts for special people. Not only you will give something that will be useful for them, you also show them that they are special.

In this book, I will give you 25 practical ideas for neat crochet projects, especially for hats and scarves. Those DIY ideas can be made during your free time so that you will have some pretty, some elegant, and some functional collections for the next autumn and winter. Be prepared to see awesomely beautiful designs and practice your crocheting skills from various different levels of expertise.

Enjoy the book and choose the one — or even some designs that attract you the most. After all, happy crocheting!!!

Chapter 1 – Before You Start

Before you start looking at the 25 beautiful hat and scarf designs, it is better to give you some basic information about the kinds of yarn and crocheting knots used in this book.

Kinds of Yarn

To choose the yarn for a perfect crocheting project, you need to consider:

- its absorbency to determine its ability to absorb sweat and possibility for warm weather wear,

- its resiliency or elasticity to make sure that it will return back to its actual size after being stretched or worn,

- its breathability to determine whether or not air can pass through the fiber,

- its softness or roughness, depending upon the functions of the finished products, and

- its thickness, which is the diameter of the yarn in micrometers.

In addition, based on the materials used to create the yarn, there are several options that you can choose, including:

1. Cotton yarn. This type of yarn usually has poor elasticity which is needed to create projects that need structure, such as bags, purse,

broche and other accessories. This kind of yarn is not soft so that it is not too good to be used as scarves. However, so people like to use this yarn for hats since it will keep the hats in shape.

2. Plant-based fibers. This type of yarn includes linen and bamboo bast. Linen has strong and warm characteristics, making it suitable for winter accessories. On the other hand, bamboo bast looks good and elegant for its natural sheen.

3. Animal-based fibers. Wool, cashmere, alpaca, and silk are included in this category. Wool is soft, softer than cotton in fact, but certain wool type is scratchy so that it is not suitable for scarves. In addition, cashmere is expensive, soft, luxurious and elegant, which is suitable for scarves. Alpaca is a great choice for winter outfit, whereas silk is very strong and suitable for summer wear.

4. Synthetic fibers. The first one is Acrylic. It is less expensive, so it becomes a perfect choice for those who just start the crocheting hobby. Acrylic yarn can also be washed easily, making it less difficult to maintain. The next type that is commonly used is nylon. Nylon thread is strong, elastic, and easy to clean or wash. The last is rayon yarn, which is inexpensive and highly absorbent. It also has beautiful natural sheen.

Size of Yarn

Please note that crochetting yarn has sizes, which is indicated by numbers. The bigger the number, the smaller the size (diameter) of the yarn. The smaller the number, the bigger the size and the easier to handle. If your level is still beginner to intermediate, I strongly suggest you to choose the small number.

Here is the guidelines to choose the right yarn size, including the size of hook needs to work on the threads.

Category Name (Symbol)	Commonly used for	Thread sizes	Hook Size (US based measurement)
Lace (0)	Cobweb, lace, crochet thread	33 to 40	000 to 1
Super Fine (1)	Sock, fingering, baby	27 to 32	1 to 3
Fine (2)	Sport, baby	23 to 26	3 to 5
Light (3)	DK, light worsted	21 to 24	5 to 6
Medium (4)	Worsted, afghan, aran	16 to 20	7 to 9
Bulky (5)	Chunky, craft, rug	12 to 15	9 to 11
Super Bulky (6)	Bulky, roving	7 to 11	11 to 17
Jumbo (7)		6 or less	17 or larger

Crocheting Abbreviations

To avoid confusions, I also write some US abbreviation for crocheting. You can always refer to this abbreviation while following the instruction given in every crochet idea.

beg   : beginning
BLO or BL: Back Loop Only - Back Loop BPdc   : back post double crochet CC   : contrasting colour ch(s)   : chain stitch(es)
CRDC   : crossed double crochet dc   : double crochet
dec   : decrease
dtr   : double treble crochet FLO or FL: Front Loop Only - Front Loop
FPdc   : front post double crochet hdc   : half double crochet
inc   : increase
lp st   : loop stitch
lp(s)   : loop(s)
MC   : Magic Circle
MC   : magic circle
Rep   : repeat
Rev   : Reverse
reverse sc: reverse single crochet rnd(s)   : round(s)
rs   : right side
sc   : single crochet
sk   : skip
sl st   : slip stitch
sp(s)   : space(s)
st(s)   : stitch(es)

tog	: together		
tr tr	: triple treble crochet	tr	: treble crochet
ws	: wrong side		
yo	: yarn over		

Head Measurements

For a baby age 1 or below:

- Head circumference = 16-19 inches
- Hat height = 7.5 inches

For a baby age 2-3 or below:

- Head circumference = 18-20 inches
- Hat height = 8 inches

For kids age 3-10:

- Head circumference = 19-20.5 inches
- Hat height = 8.5 inches

For teenagers age 11-19:

- Head circumference = 20.5-22 inches
- Hat height = 9-10 inches

For Adult woman:

- Head circumference = 21.5-22.5 inches
- Hat height = 11 inches

For Adult man:

- Head circumference = 23-24 inches
- Hat height = 11-11.5 inches

Chapter 2 – Ideas for Hats

In this chapter, you will have some great ideas on hats for adults and kids.

Hat Ideas for Adults

#1. Unisex Brimmed Hat

Because brim can protect you from the sun and it adds an element of awesomeness, some people prefer to have the brim in their hat. Here is the tutorial to make a unisex brimmed hat.

HOOK: 5 mm

YARN WEIGHT: Medium (4) **MATERIALS**:

- 1 ball of soft yarn with the choice of color that can be suitable for both man and woman (for example grey, beige, navy blue, or brown)

- plastic for brim

- Stitch marker

- Yarn needle

GAUGE: 16 sc = 4"; 15 rows = 4"

INSTRUCTIONS:

Hat is worked in continuous rounds. You need to place marker in the beginning of the round.

For the Crown:

Ch 4, slip st in first ch to form ring. Place marker in the beginning of round.

Rnd 1: Work 6 sc in ring – 6 sts.

Rnd 2: Work 2 sc in each st around – 12 sts.

Rnd 3: [2 sc in next st, sc in next st] – 18 sts.

Rnd 4: [2 sc in next st, sc in next 2 sts] – 24 sts.

Rnd 5: [2 sc in next st, sc in next 3 sts] – 30 sts.

Rnd 6: [2 sc in next st, sc in next 4 sts] – 36 sts.

Rnd 7: [2 sc in next st, sc in next 5 sts] – 42 sts.

Rnd 8: [2 sc in next st, sc in next 6 sts] – 48 sts.

Rnd 9: Ch 3 (counts as dc here and throughout), dc in same space, dc in next 7 sts, [2 dc in next st, dc in next 7 sts] – 54 sts.

Rnd 10: [2 sc in next st, sc in next 8 sts] – 60 sts. Rnd 11: [2 sc in next st, sc in next 9 sts] – 66 sts. Rnd 12: [2 sc in next st, sc in next 10 sts] – 72 sts.

Rnd 13: [2 sc in next st, sc in next11 sts] – 78 sts.

Rnd 14: Ch 3, dc in each st around.

Rnds 15-18: Sc in each st around.

Rnds 19-28: Repeat Rounds 14-18.

Rnd 29: Hdc in each st around, slip st in first st. Fasten off.

For the Brim:

Top Side Mark 22 sts on front of Hat on Rnd 29 for Brim.

Row 1: With right side facing, join yarn in first marked st, working in front loops only, sc in each next 22 sts.

Row 2: Ch 1, turn, sc in each st across, sc in BL in next 4 sts on Hat – 26 sts.

Row 3: Ch 1, turn, sc in each st across, sc in FL in next 4 sts on Hat – 30 sts.

Row 4: Ch 1, turn, sc in each st across, sc in BL in next st on Hat – 31 sts.

Row 5: Ch 1, turn, sc in each st across, sc in FL in next st on Hat – 32

Row 6: Ch 1, turn, sc in each st across, sc in BL in next st on Hat – 33 sts.

Row 7: Ch 1, turn, sc in each st across, sc in FL in next st on Hat – 34 sts. Fasten off.

For the Bottom Side:

Row 1: With ws facing, join yarn on ws of Row 1 of Brim, sc in BL of first 22 sts.

Row 2: Ch 1, turn, sc in each st across, sc in FL in next 4 sts on Hat – 26 sts.

Row 3: Ch 1, turn, sc in each st across, sc in BL in next 4 sts on Hat – 30 sts.

Row 4: Ch 1, turn, sc in each st across, sc in FL in next st on Hat – 31 sts.

Row 5: Ch 1, turn, sc in each st across, sc in BL in next st on Hat – 32 sts.

Row 6: Ch 1, turn, sc in each st across, sc in FL in next st on Hat – 33 sts.

Row 7: Ch 1, turn, sc in each st across, sc in BL in next st on Hat – 34 sts.

Fasten off.

Strengthening the Brim:

cut a piece of stiff interfacing or plastic in the same size with the brim. You can use the brim to create the pattern. Slip in the plastic between layers of Brim and sew Brim closed. Weave in ends.

#2. Simple Beanie Hats

This is the simple beanie hat that crafter at any level can make. One advantage of making the simple beanie hat is that you can add accessories, such as flowers, on it. In addition, to create a more colorful touch, you can also choose rainbow yarn or yarns in several different colors.

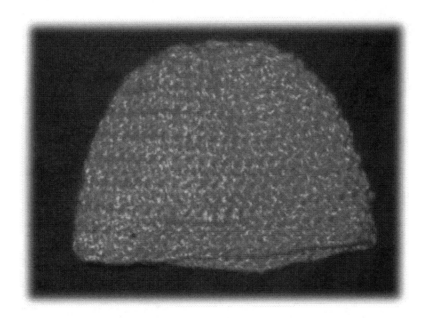

HOOK: 5 mm

YARN: Medium (4)

MATERIALS:

- Yarn of your favorite color

INSTRUCTION:

Rnd 1: chain 5, slip stitch in 5th from hook, 10 d.c. in loop, place marker Rnd 2: 3 dc. in each dc. Around

Rnd 3: 2 dc. in next dc., dc. in next dc around

Rnd 4: 2 dc. in next dc., dc. in next 2 dc. Around Rnd 5: 2 dc. in next dc., dc. in next 3 dc. Around Rnd 6: 2 dc. in next dc., dc. in next 4 dc. Around Rnd 7 – 15: dc. in each dc. Around

Finish off.

#3. News Boy Hat with Strap

The newsboy hat is always a favorite. With its brimmed decoration for a more stylish look, the hat looks amazing to be worn both in day time or evening outing.

One feature that will be presented here is the strap added at the front part of the hat with a big button in every side of the strap.

MATERIALS:

- Yarn: Medium (4) in your favorite color

- Hook: 5 mm

- 2 pieces of ¾" or 1" buttons

- Gauge: 14 stiches and 11 rows = 4" (10cm)

INSTRUCTIONS:

Head Circumference = 22" − 23"

Hat Circumference = 20.5"

Hat Height = 8.25"

Rnd 1: Chain 2, make 8 half double crochet in the 2nd chain from hook, sl st to join in first half double crochet (8) Rnd 2: Chain 1, make 2 half double crochet in each stitch around, join (16) Rnd 3: Chain 1, in first stitch *make 2 half double crochet, half double crochet in next stitch* repeat around, join (24) Rnd 4: Chain 1, in first stitch *make 2 half double crochet, half double crochet in next 2 stitches* repeat around, join (32) Rnd 5: Chain 1, in first stitch *make 2 half double crochet, half double crochet in next 3 stitches* repeat around, join (40) Rnd 6: Chain 1, in first stitch *make 2 half double crochet, half double crochet in next 4 stitches* repeat around, join (48) Rnd 7: Chain 1, in first stitch *make 2 half double crochet, half double crochet in next 5 stitches* repeat around, join (56) Rnd 8: Chain 1, in first stitch *make 2 half double crochet, half double crochet in next 6 stitches* repeat around, join (64) Rnd 9: Chain 1, in first stitch *make 2 half double crochet, half double crochet in next 15 stitches* repeat around, join (68)

Visor:

With the right side of the hat facing you, locate the front 26 stitches and join in the rightmost stitch.

Row 1: Chain 1, make 1 half double crochet in the same stitch, half double crochet in the next 25 stitches, turn (26) Row 2: Skip 1 stitch, single crochet in next 2 stitches, *make 2 single crochet in next stitch, sc in next 2 stitches* repeat between * until 2 stitches remain, single crochet 2together, turn (31) Row 3: Skip 1 stitch, half double crochet in next stitch, half double crochet in next 27 stitches, half double crochet2together, do not turn, continue with final round of single crochet (29)

Final Round of single crochet:

Slip stitch in the same place as the last stitch of Row 3, sc at the end of the next two rows then continue crossing around the hat making 1 single crochet in each stitch.

When you get back to the visor, create 1 single crochet in the end of each row and in each half double crochet across the front of the visor back to where you started. Join in the first stitch and then fasten off.

Button Band:

Chain 35, make 3 half double crochet in the 2nd chain from the hook, half double crochet in each chain to the end, make 5 half double crochet in the last chain —working the opposite side of the chain – half double crochet in each chain across, make 2 half double crochet in the last chain (same space as the first 3 half double crochet), join in first stitch and fasten off, leaving a lengthy tail.

Use the tail to sew the band on above the visor. Sew a button (or whatever accessory you want) to each end of the band.

#4. Basic Hat with Ear Flaps

To protect you from the cold, ear flaps are often chosen as a crochet hat accessory. Here is the easiest crochet hat with ear flaps.

INSTRUCTIONS:

Head Circumference = 22" – 23"

Hat Circumference = 20.5"

Hat Height = 8.25"

Rnd 1: Chain 2, make 8 half double crochet in the 2nd chain from hook, and then join in first half double crochet (8) Rnd 2: Chain 1, make 2 half double crochet in each stitch around, and then join (16) Rnd 3: Chain 1, in first stitch *make 2 half double crochet, half double crochet in next stitch* rep around, and then join (24) Rnd 4: Chain 1, in first stitch *make 2 half double crochet, half double crochet in next 2 stitches* rep around, and then join (32) Rnd 5: Chain 1, in first stitch *make 2 half double crochet, half double crochet in next 3 stitches* rep around, and then join (40) Rnd 6: Chain 1, in first stitch *make 2 half double crochet, half double crochet in next 4 stitches* rep around, and then join (48) Rnd

7: Chain 1, in first stitch *make 2 half double crochet, half double crochet in next 5 stitches* rep around, and then join (56) Rnd 8: Chain 1, in first stitch *make 2 half double crochet, half double crochet in next 6 stitches* rep around, and then join (64) Rnd 9: Chain 1, in first stitch *make 2 half double crochet, half double crochet in next 7 stitches* rep around, and then join (72) Rnd 10 to 22: Chain 1, half double crochet in each stitch around, and then join (72) **Ear Flap # 1:** Join in the 11th stitch from the starting seam.

(Ch 1 does not count as a stitch; do not work into it.) Row 1: Chain 1, (sc) single crochet in same stitch, sc in next 11 stitches, turn (12) Row 2: Chain 1, (sc) single crochet in first stitch and each stitch across, turn (12) Row 3: Chain 1, skip first stitch, (sc) single crochet in the next stitch and in each stitch across, turn (11) Row 4: Chain 1, skip first stitch, (sc) single crochet in the next stitch and in each stitch across, turn (10) Row 5: Chain 1, skip first stitch, (sc) single crochet in the next stitch and in each stitch across, turn (9) Row 6: Chain 1, skip first stitch, (sc) single crochet in the next stitch and in each stitch across, turn (8) Row 7: Chain 1, skip first stitch, (sc) single crochet in the next stitch and in each stitch across, turn (7) Row 8: Chain 1, skip first stitch, (sc) single crochet in the next stitch and in each stitch across, turn (6) Row 9: Chain 1, skip first stitch, (sc) single crochet in the next stitch and in each stitch across, turn (5) Row 10: Chain 1, skip first stitch, (sc) single crochet in the next stitch and in each stitch across, turn (4) Row 11: Chain 1, skip first stitch, (sc) single crochet in the next 3 stitches, fasten off (3) **Ear Flap #2:** Leave 27 stitches unworked and then join in the 28th stitch. Rep the steps in Ear Flap #1 – yet, do not fasten off after the last row; continue working around the hat making 1 single crochet in each stitch including the ends of each Ear Flap row.

Reaching the tip of the Ear Flap, you need to make the first tie: Ch 51, sl-st in the 2nd chain from the hook, slip stitch in each chain back to the Ear Flap, slip stitch into the same space as the last sc on the Ear Flap, single crochet in the next stitch and continue working around the hat.

Rep the tie step on the other Ear Flap.

Fasten off and weave in all ends only after you reach the starting point.

#5. Pretty Easy Slouchy Hat

Both men and women (especially teenagers and young adults) just love this fashionable slouchy hat. No need to explain further why, you know the reasons.

MATERIALS:

- Hook sizes K (6.5mm), H(5.0mm), G(4.25mm)

- Yarn needle

- Medium Yarn (4)

- Stitch marker

GAUGE: 5 HDC x 3 rows = 1.5" square **INSTRUCTIONS:**

Rnd 1: 10 HDC in MC (10)

Rnd 2: 2 HDC in each ST around (20)

Rnd 3: 2 HDC in each ST around (40)

Rnd 4: (2 HDC in next, 1 HDC in next) around (60) Rnd 5: (2 HDC in next, 1 HDC in next, 1 HDC in next) around (80) Switch to H hook.

Rnd 6: CRDC around (you will complete 40 CRDC for a total of 80 ST) Rnd 7: Skip 1st stitch (this will stagger your CRDCs, which gives your hat a diagonal look). CRDC around Rnd 8: CRDC around. (You will complete 40 CRDC for a total of 80 ST) Rnd 9-16: Repeat Round 8

Switch to G Hook.

Rnd 17: CRDC around, skipping one stitch after every 2 CRDCs until you reach end of round (you will complete 32 CRDC for a total of 64 ST) Rnd 18: SC around (64)

Rnd 19-26: Repeat Round 18

When you complete Rnd 26, make 5 slip stitches (SS); fasten off and weave in ends.

#6. Lady-Like Crochet Hat

This crochet hat is one of my favorite because it looks so elegant and reminds me of the style of ladies in the black and white movies.

MATERIALS:

137 yards of bulky weight yarn (5)

Hook: Size J (6.00 mm) and Size K (6.5 mm)

Brooch or button (optional)

INSTRUCTIONS:

Rnd 1: 8 hdc into a magic loop, slip to join, ch 2 (does not count as stitch, do not turn your work until otherwise instructed) Rnd 2: 2 hdc in each stitch around, slip to join, ch 2 (16) Rnd 3: *hdc, 2 hdc in next* around, slip to join, ch 2 (24) Rnd 4:*hdc 2, 2 hdc in next* around, slip to join, ch 2 (32) Rnd 5:*hdc 3, 2 hdc in next* around, slip to join, ch 2 (40) Rnd 6:*hdc 4 2 hdc in next* around, slip to join, ch 2 (48) Rnd 7:*hdc 5, 2 hdc* around, slip to join, ch 2 (56) Rnd 8:hdc around, slip to join, ch 2

Rnd 9:hdc around, slip to join, ch 2

Rnd 10:hdc around, slip to join, ch 2

Rnd 11:hdc around, slip to join, ch 2

Rnd 12:hdc around, slip to join, ch 2

Rnd 13:hdc around, slip to join, ch 2

Rnd 14:hdc around, slip to join, ch 2

Rnd 15:hdc around, slip to join, ch 2

Rnd 16:hdc around, slip to join, ch 2

Rnd 17:hdc around, slip to join, ch 3

Switch to size "K" hook, (dc2, ch, dc 2) in first, *skip 2, (dc 2, ch, dc 2) in next* repeat until one stitch remains, skip it, slip to join, ch 3 and turn Rnd 18: (dc 2, ch, dc 2) in each ch space from previous round, slip to join, ch 3 and turn.

Rnd 19: (dc 2, ch, dc 2) in each ch space from previous round, slip to join, ch 3 and turn.

Rnd 20: (dc 2, ch, dc 2) in each ch space from previous round, slip to join, ch 3 and turn.

Rnd 21: (dc 2, ch, dc 2) in each ch space from previous round, slip to join, ch 3 and turn.

Rnd 22: (dc 2, ch, dc 2) in each ch space from previous round, slip to join, ch 3 and turn. Bind off and weave in ends.

Fold one side of the brim up and secure with a brooch.

#7. Snowflakes Pin Hat

One great feature that I particularly like about this design is the snowflake is made separately as a pin, so that you can change it with other ornaments or designs (like flower pin or animal pin) in other season than winter.

MATERIALS

Yarn: Medium (4)
Hook: Size G (4.5mm) and size H (5mm)

Adjust your hook size to achieve gauge as listed below.

Gauge:

8 sc and 9 rnds = 2"; use G (4.5mm) hook.

7 hdc and 5 rnds = 2"; use H (5mm) hook.

Tapestry needle

Pin (to attach the snowflake)

INSTRUCTIONS:

Slouch Hat Pattern

Using mc yarn and larger hook, ch 2 loosely.

Foundation Rnd: 6 sc into 2nd ch from hook, sl st to 1st sc to close rnd -- 6 sts.

Rnd 1: Ch 2 (counts as 1st hdc), 1 hdc in same st, *2 hdc in next st; rep from* around, sl st to end -- 12 sts.

Rnd 2: Ch 2, 1 hdc in same st, *2 hdc in next st; rep from* around, sl st to end -- 24 sts.

Rnd 3: Ch 2, 1 hdc in same st, 1 hdc in next st, *2 hdc in next st, 1 hdc in next st; rep from* around, sl st to end -- 36 sts.

Rnd 4: Ch 2, 1 hdc in same st, 1 hdc in next 2 sts, *2 hdc in next st, 1 hdc in next 2 sts; rep from* around, sl st to end -- 48 sts.

Rnd 5: Ch 2, 1 hdc in same st, 1 hdc in next 3 sts, *2 hdc in next st, 1 hdc in next 3 sts; rep from* around, sl st to end -- 60 sts.

Rnd 6: Ch 2, 1 hdc in same st, 1 hdc in next 9 sts, *2 hdc in next st, 1 hdc in next 9 sts; rep from* around, sl st to end -- 66 sts.

Rnd 7: Ch 2, 1 hdc in same st, 1 hdc in next 10 sts, *2 hdc in next st, 1 hdc in next 10 sts; rep from* around, sl st to end -- 72 sts.

Stop increasing here for size Small/18" only and proceed to Rnd 10.

Rnd 8: Ch 2, 1 hdc in same st, 1 hdc in next 11 sts, *2 hdc in next st, 1 hdc in next 11 sts; rep from* around, sl st to end -- 78 sts.

Stop increasing here for size Medium/19.5" only and proceed to Rnd 10.

Rnd 9: Ch 2, 1 hdc in same st, 1 hdc in next 12 sts, *2 hdc in next st, 1 hdc in next 12 sts; rep from* around, sl st to end -- 84 sts.

Stop increasing here for size Large/21" only and proceed to Rnd 10.

Rnd 10 (All Sizes): Ch 2, 1 hdc in each st around, sl st to beg ch to end -- 72 (78, 84) sts.

*Repeat Rnd 10 until hat measures 6 (6.5, 6.5)" from center top of crown, or until desired length before forehead band.

Change to smaller crochet hook.

Rnd 11: Ch 1, 1 sc in each st around, sl st to beg ch to end -- 72 (78, 84) sts.

***Repeat Rnd 11 for 1.5 (2, 2)".**

Rnd 12: Ch 1, 1 sc in same st, 1 sc in next 5 sts, *2 sc in next st, 1 sc in next 5 sts; rep from* 10 (11, 12) times more -- 84 (91, 98) sts.

Rnd 13: Ch 1, 1 sc in same st, 1 sc in next 6 sts, *2 sc in next st, 1 sc in next 6 sts; rep from* 10 (11, 12) times more -- 96 (104, 112) sts.

Change to cc yarn.

Rnd 14 (Last Rnd): Ch 1, 1 sc in each st around, sl st to beg ch to end -- 96 (104, 112) sts.

Fasten off and weave in ends.

Snowflake Pin

Using cc yarn and smaller hook, ch 4, sl st in 1st ch to form ring.

Foundation Rnd: Ch 1 (counts as 1st sc), 11 sc into center of ring, sl st to beginning ch to end -- 12 sc.

Rnd 1: *Ch 5, sk next sc, sl st in next sc; rep from* 5 times more -- 6 ch-5 sps.

Rnd 2: *ch 3, [ch 3, sc in 3rd ch from hook] 3 times to create 3 picots, work 1 sc in each of the 3 ch sts created immediately before the picots, 2 sc in next ch-5 sp, ch 2, sc in ch-5 sp, ch 3, sc in ch-5 sp, ch 2, 2 sc in ch-5 sp, sl st in next sl st; rep from* 5 times more.

Fasten off and weave in ends.

Finishing

Sew snowflake applique directly to cloche as shown in photos or to a pin as desired.

Weave in and trim all remaining yarn ends.

Hat Ideas for Kids

#8. Newsboy Hat with Strap and Button

For the materials, refer to the idea #3.

INSTRUCTION:

Head Circumference = 18″ − 20″

Rnd 1: Chain 2, make 8 half double crochet in the 2nd chain from hook, sl stitch to join in first half double crochet (8) Rnd 2: Chain 1, make 2 half double crochet in each stitch around, join (16)

Rnd 3: Chain 1, in first stitch *make 2 half double crochet, half double crochet in next stitch* repeat around, join (24) Rnd 4: Chain 1, in first stitch *make 2 half double crochet, half double crochet in next 2 stitches* repeat around, join (32) Rnd 5: Chain 1, in first stitch *make 2 half double crochet, half double crochet in next 3 stitches* repeat around, join (40) Rnd 6: Chain 1, in first stitch *make 2 half double crochet, half double crochet in next 4 stitches* repeat around, join (48) Rnd 7: Chain 1, in first stitch *make 2 half double crochet, half double crochet in next 11 stitches* repeat around, join (52) Rnd 8: Chain 1, in first stitch *make 2 half double crochet, half double crochet in next 6 stitches* repeat around, join (64) Rnd 9 to 21: Chain 1, half double crochet in each stitch around, join (64) Fasten off.

Visor:

Do this with the right side of the fancy hat facing directly to you and then locate the front 24 stitches and join in the rightmost stitch.

R 1: Chain 1, make 1 half double crochet in the same stitch, half double crochet in the next 23 stitches, turn (24) R 2: Skip 1 stitch, *single crochet in next 2 stitches, 2 single crochet in next stitch* repeat between * until 2 stitches remain, single crochet2together, turn (28) R 3: Skip 1 stitch, half double crochet in next stitch, half double crochet in next 24 stitches, half double crochet2together, do not turn, continue with final round of single crochet (26) **Final Round of Single Crochet:**
Slip stitch in the same space as the last stitch of Row 3, single crochet in the end of the next two rows and continue crossing around the hat making 1 single crochet in each stitch.

When you get back to the visor, make 1 single crochet in the end of each row and in each half double crochet across the front of the visor back to where you started. Join in the first stitch and then fasten off.

Button:

Chain 33, make 3 single crochet in the 2nd chain from the hook, sc in each chain to the end, make 5 sc in the last chain – working the opposite side of the chain – sc in each chain across, make 2 sc in the last chain (same space as the first 3 sc), join in first stitch and fasten off, leaving a lengthy tail. Use the tail to sew the band on above the visor. Sew a button on each end of the band.

#9. Cute Monkey Hat with Ear Flaps (For 4-10 years old)

MATERIALS:

- Yarn: Medium (4) with three different color of your choice (Color A, Color B, Color C)

- Hook: 5.0 mm (H-8)

- 2 pcs of ¾ " buttons

- Stitch marker for keeping track of rounds

- Yarn needle for weaving in ends

INSTRUCTION

Head Circumference = 18″ – 20″

Hat Circumference= 18″

Hat Height = 7.75″

Rnd 1: **With Color A** – Chain 2, make 8 half double crochet in the 2nd chain from hook, join in first half double crochet (8) Rnd 2: Chain 1, make 2 half double crochet in each stitch around, join (16)

Rnd 3: Chain 1, in first stitch *make 2 half double crochet, half double crochet in next stitch* repeat around, join (24) Rnd 4: Chain 1, in first stitch *make 2 half double crochet, half double crochet in next 2 stitches* repeat around, join (32) Rnd 5: Chain 1, in first stitch *make 2 half double crochet, half double crochet in next 3 stitches* repeat around, join (40) Rnd 6: Chain 1, in first stitch *make 2 half double crochet, half double crochet in next 4 stitches* repeat around, join (48) Rnd 7: Chain 1, in first stitch *make 2 half double crochet, half double crochet in next 5 stitches* repeat around, join (56) Rnd 8: **With Color B** – Ch 1, in first stitch *make 2 half double crochet, half double crochet in next 6 stitches* repeat around, join (64) Rnd 9 to 21: **With Color C** – Ch 1, half double crochet in each stitch around, join (64) At this point the hat should measure approximately 7.5″ in height. Adjust the number of rounds if needed and fasten off.

Ear Flap # 1: Join Color C in the 10th stitch from the starting seam. (Chain 1 does not count as a stitch; do not work into it.) Row 1: Chain 1, single crochet in same stitch, single crochet in next 10 stitches, turn (11) Row 2: Chain 1, single crochet in first stitch and each stitch across, turn (11)

Row 3: Chain 1, skip first stitch, sc in the next stitch and in each stitch across, turn (10) Row 4: Chain 1, skip first stitch, sc in the next stitch and in each stitch across, turn (9) Row 5: Chain 1, skip first stitch, sc in the next stitch and in each stitch across, turn (8) Row 6: Chain 1, skip first stitch, sc in the next stitch and in each stitch across, turn (7) Row 7: Chain 1, skip first stitch, sc in the next stitch and in each stitch across, turn (6) Row 8: Chain 1, skip first stitch, sc in the next stitch and in each stitch across, turn (5) Row 9: Chain 1, skip first stitch, sc in the next stitch, sc2together, sc in the last stitch, fasten off (3) **Ear Flap #2:** Leave 23 stitches unworked and then join Color C in the 24th stitch. After that, rep the steps from Ear Flap #1.

Final Round:

Join the Color B at the hat seam, chain1, make 1 single crochet in each stitch around the hat, when you reach the first Ear Flap, make 1 sc in the end of each row. On the last row of the flap, make 1 single crochet in the first stitch, in the next stitch make [single crochet, chain 2, single crochet] (this makes a space for attaching the braids), make 1 sc in the next stitch and continue working around the hat.

Rep the above steps on the other Ear Flap. Continue making 1 single crochet in each stitch back to start, join in first sc and fasten off.

#10. Elsa Crochet Hat

This is girls ' favorite cartoon character of the century. To please your little daughter, why don ' t you make her this beautiful Elsa Crochet Hat?

INSTRUCTIONS:

For the Hat

Rnd 1: Magic ring, chain 2, 10 double crochet into a magic ring, slip stitch into top of chain 2.   (11) Rnd 2: chain 2, double crochet into base of chain, 2 dc in all stitches, slip stitch into top of ch 2.   (22) Rnd 3: chain 2, 2 double crochet into the next stitch, *double crochet, 2 double crochet* repeat around, slip stitch into top of ch 2.   (33) Rnd 4: chain 2, double crochet into the first stitch, 2 double crochet into the next stitch, *dc, dc, 2 dc* repeat around slst into top of ch 2.   (44) Rnd 5: chain 2, double crochet into the next two stitches, 2 double crochet into the next stitch, *dc, dc, dc, 2 dc* repeat around slst into top of chain 2.   (55) Rnd 6 – 10: ch2, double crochet into each stitch, slst into top of chain 2.

Rnd 11: {Color change} ch1, single crochet into each stitch, slip stitch into top of chain 1.

For the Hair

Cut the yarn two times longer than the hair length you want to make then folded in half to place into the hat.

To attach the hair to the hat, take two strands, fold in half, finding the middle. Using a crochet hook, slip hook into the bottom stitch from the bottom of the hat toward the top. Hook the middle of the hair pieces and pull a couple of inches through.

Then pass the long end of the strands through the loop you just created and pull tight. Repeat around. After that gather all hair behind left ear and braid one long braid. I parted it on the front left above the eye. Tight the braids with hair ties or yarn.

Chapter 3 – Ideas for Scarves

In this chapter, you will have some great ideas on scarves for women, men, and kids.

Scarf Ideas for Women

#11. Elegant Infinity Scarf

This scarf is simple and elegant. If you don ' t want to spend a long time to make a scarf project, you can choose this pattern. Most people will finish the scarf in less than 5 hours. The thicker the yarn, the bigger the hook, the shorter the time to make it. The final result of the scarf will highly depends on the character of your yarn and hook.

Finished size: 11" wide x 42" long **INSTRUCTIONS:**

Ch 25

Row 1: Work sc in each ch space, ch 2, turn Row 2: Work dc in each sc, ch 1, turn Row 3: Work sc in each loop of each dc (not in the ch space), ch 1, turn Row 4: Work sc in each ch space of each sc, ch 2, turn Repeat rows 2-4 until you run out of yarn or until the scarf is as long as you like.

Seam the two edges together.

Weave in ends.

#12. My Favorite Multicolor Scarf

This is my favorite scarf. I love the color combinations that make it suitable to be worn in any season and almost any kinds of outfit. Moreover, you can use any leftover yarns to make this scarf (as long as the color match)

INSTRUCTIONS

Leaving at least a 15 cm (6 inch) tail, ch 40.

Row 1: Double crochet 2 in 4th ch from hook, *skip 3, (dc 1, ch 2, dc 1) in next stitch, sk 3, (dc 2, ch 1, dc 2) in next st, repeat from* across, ending row with sk 3 (dc 1, ch 1, dc 1) in last chain, turn.

Row 2: Chain 3, dc 2 in first ch-1-sp, *(dc 1, ch 2, dc 1) in next ch-1-sp, (dc 2, ch*

1, dc 2) in next ch-2- sp, repeat from across, ending row with dc 1 in sp between 2 dc and turning chain, chain 1, dc 1 in top ch of turning chain, turn.

Repeat row 2 for pattern until scarf measures approx. 175 cm (69 inches) or until you run out of yarn. Fasten off, leaving a tail of at least 15 cm (6 inches).

FINISHING

If you want to omit the fringe, weave in ends.

Otherwise, count ends as strands to be incorporated into the fringe. Wash and block as desired.

Using the cut strands of yarn * hold 5 strands together, fold them in half. With WS of the scarf facing you insert hook in bottom edge, pull loop through, pull all 10 strands through loop on hook and tighten.

Repeat from * 12 more times evenly across bottom edge.

Repeat for top edge.

#13. Puffy Warm Winter Scarf

Puffy scarf is easy to make and suitable for cold weather. You have no reason for not making one. One great tip: use colorful yarns.

People usually choose natural or pale color for winter outfit — which I personally thing as adding gloomier atmosphere to the winter. So, why don't you think of making the warmer in the touch of summer?

INSTRUCTIONS:

To make the puff stitch:

Yarn over, insert hook in indicated stitch and draw up a loop (3 loops on hook), [yarn over, insert hook in same stitch and draw up a loop] 3 times (9 loops on hook), yarn over and draw through first 8 loops on hook, yarn over and draw through remaining 2 loops on hook.

Chain 26.

Rnd 1: Work puff stitch in fourth chain from hook. *Ch 1, skip next ch, puff stitch in next ch,* rep 11 times (12 puff sts).

Rnd 2: Ch 3, turn. *Puff stitch in next ch-1 sp, ch 1,* rep 11 times. Puff stitch in last ch-3 space (12 puff sts).

Repeat Row 2 until desired length (for example: Row 150 or 94"). Finish off and weave in ends.

#14. Lightweight Chain Summer Scarf

Who said that scarf is made for winter only. Summer scarf is not a bad idea to spice up your hot looking summer outfits.

INSTRUCTIONS:

36 Foundation HDC

Row 1: Ch 1, turn, 36 HDC

Rows 2 & 3: Repeat row 1. Weave in tail end, and Slst across two short sides to form a loop.

FINISHING: Repeat rows 1-3 for 12 more times (or on your desired length), connect each chain around each other. Connect the 13th link to both ends to make the scarf infinite.

#15. Beautiful Triangle Spring Scarf

This idea will challenge you to use smaller size of yarn, improving your crocheting skills while creating something beautiful for your spring evenings.

You have to make two parts and then connect them together to make this scarf. The first part in the Lace pattern, and the second part is the edging.

INSTRUCTIONS:

For the Lace Pattern

Start working by creating a chain 386 + 1. Or, you can make a Foundation Single Crochet 386 and skip Row 1

R1: Make single crochet in the second chain. After that, create single crochet in each chain until the end of 386 stitches.

R2: Chain 5 (make sure to count), and then turn to this formula [skip3 stitches, *single crochet, chain 3, repeat the formula 2 more times, single crochet, chain 3, sk3 stitches, (double crochet, chain2, double crochet).

Next stitch, chain 3] repeat 33times, skip 3 stitches, *sc, ch3. Repeat from (*) 2 more times, single crochet, chain3, skip 3 stitches, double crochet in final stitch. Repeat this step (*) for 35 patterns in total R3: chain 4, skip first 2 chain-spaces, (double crochet, chain2, double crochet) into next chain spaces, *ch3, sk2 chain spaces, (sc, ch3, sc, ch3, sc, ch3, sc) into next chain spaces (between double chain's), ch3, sk2 ch-sps, (dc, ch2, dc) into the ch sp and repeat from () to end.*

Finish with a double treble crochet into either chain 5 (1st row 3) or chain 2 space between double crochet's (all remaining repeats). Turn work and slip-stitches into double treble crochet just made, sl-st into ch2 sp, single crochet into ch2 sp.

Repeat R 3 until the your work has decreased to the penultimate row – there will be two sets of (double crochet, chain2, double crochet).

R4:: chain 4, skip first 2 chain-spaces, (double crochet, chain2, double crochet), into next chain space (the central chain-space), ch4, skip 2 chain-spaces, sling stitch into final chain space and then fasten off.

Edging

The edge is also divided into two sections, the mesh and the picoted edge.

The mesh

The mesh is made by working 2 double crochet into every chain for 4 space, and 1 double crochet into every chain2 space as you work along the edge. The double crochet's are separated by a chain2.

For this foundation row, you need to re-join the yarn until the end of the edge R1: Chain3 (counts as 1double crochet, chain1), double crochet in same space, chain 2, double crochet in top of chain3 of the first row in the main body, chain2, double crochet in chain2 space. *chain2, double crochet, repeat from ()* along the edge then working 2double crochet in every chain4 space (double treble crochet post counts as chain 4) and 1 double crochet into each chain 2 space.

At the central chain space, work 2double crochet (separated by a chhain2) and then continue along the second edge until 2 chain space. Make a double crochet into a chain2 space.

Chain2, double crochet into next chain space, chain2, double crochet into the corner of the foundation row, chain1, double crochet. (211 chain-spaces) R2:

Chain5 (counts as double crochet, chain2), turn, double crochet in next double crochet, *chain2, double crochet in next double crochet, repeat till centre chain-space, chain2, double crochet in centre chain-space, chain2, double crochet in very next double crochet*, chain2, double crochet in next double crochet, repeat to end (212 chain-spaces).

R3: Chain5, turn, double crochet in same stitch, *chain2, double crochet in next double crochet, repeat till centre double crochet, work an extra chain2, double crochet in central double crochet*, chain2, double crochet in next double crochet, repeat to end, chain2, double crochet in same stitch (215 chain-spaces).

The mesh is now done. The last 3 rows make the scalloped edge.

R4: chain1, turn, single crochet in same stitch. *Chain4, single crochet in next double crochet, repeat from* to end (continue to mark the centre chain-space).

R5: Chain4, turn, single crochet in chain-space, *8double crochet in next chain space, single crochet in next chain-space, chain4, single crochet in next chain-space, repeat from ()* until there is one chain-space left before the central one, 8double crochet in next chain-space, single crochet in central chain-space, 8double crochet in next chain-space, **single crochet in next chain-space, chain4, single crochet in next chain-space, 8double crochet in next chain-space, repeat from (**) until there is one chain-space remaining, single crochet in final chain-space.

Special stitch-Picot: Chain4, sling-stitch in third chain from hook, chain1

R6: Chain2, turn, double crochet in same stitch, chain4, skip first two double crochet, double crochet, picot, skip2 stitches, double crochet, *chain4, single crochet into chain-space, chain4, skip next two double crochet, double crochet, picot, skip2 stitches, double crochet, repeat from* to central stitch, chain1, picot, chain1, skip 5stitchs (two double crochet, one single crochet and two double crochet) double crochet, picot, skip 2 stitches, double crochet, chain4, single crochet into chain-space, **chain4, skip next two double crochet, double crochet, picot, skip 2 stitches, double crochet, chain4, single crochet into chain-space, repeat from ** to end.

Fasten off and after that weave in at the ends.

Finishing:

Wet blocking

#16. Buttoned Cawl

If you are running out of scarf idea, try to find one or two big buttons and create this beautiful piece. Turn your scarf into cawl.

INSTRUCTIONS:

Chain 23. Dc in 3rd chain from the hook and in each chain across. And then turn.

Row 1: Chain 3, double crochet in each Dc across, and then turn.

Rep R 1 until it measures 32" (approximately 28 rows of Double crochet).

Measure it around your neck to make sure you like the length. Tie off.

Finishing: Add the buttons.

Scarf Ideas for Men

#17. Vertical Stripe Men Scarf

The vertical stripe scarf is an item that is loved by men. If you wish to create one for your special man, try this simple scarf patter. Choose 2 colors of his favorite and start crocheting.

INSTRUCTIONS:

Make chain as long as you will like your scarf to be.

Row 1 (color A): In the fourth ch from the hook, work a dc. Work a dc in each ch across.

Row 2 (color B): Ch 3 and turn, work a bpdc (back post double crochet, see video tutorial below) into each dc across row. Work a dc in the turning chain.

Row 3 (color A): Ch 3 and turn. Work a dc into each stitch across. Work a dc in the turning chain.

Repeat rows 2 and 3 until scarf is desired width, ending on row 2 for a nice finished edge. I worked a total of 10 rows for the scarf shown. Fasten off.

#18. Hunky Ribbed Men Scarf

The scarf is the combination of simplicity and elegance. You can use one color or two colors of yarn to add details.

Make chain as long as you will like your scarf to be.

Row 1: hdc into third chain from hook and into every chain until end. chain 2 and turn.

Row 2: hdc into third loop of last hdc from previous row, which will now be on the back side of the work. hdc into third loop of every stitch from row 1 until end, and hdc into first chain of initial ch 2 of row1.

Row 3: Repeat row 2 until scarf is desired width. The scarf shown here consists of 14 rows.

#19. Army Colors Men Scarf

This macho scarf will absolutely boost the man ' s confidence.

INSTRUCTIONS:

Choose the yarn in army colors.

Ch 133. Mark every 30th ch for easier counting.

Row 1: 1 hdc in 3rd ch from hook. 1 hdc in each ch across. Turn. 131 hdc.

Row 2: Ch 2 (does not count as hdc). *Work 1 hdc in horizontal bar created between stitches of previous row (bar is below loops normally worked). Rep from* across. Turn. 131 hdc. Rep 2nd row until Scarf measures 6" [15 cm]. Fasten off.

#20. Classic British Scarf for Men

I fall in love with this item at the first sight. When I made one, it felt like a dream came true. The details are just so beautiful, especially when you choose elegant colors, like dark brown, grey, black, or navy blue.

INSTRUCTIONS:

Row 1: With Charcoal, FSC 270 (or ch 271, sc in 2nd ch from hook and across) (270 SC) Row 2: Ch 1, turn, in BLO, SC across (270 SC)

Row 3-4: Repeat Row 2

Row 5: *Ch 3, sk 3 sts, sc in next st, repeat from* Across. (68 Ch 3 spaces) Row 6:

ch 1, turn, Sc across putting 3 scs in the ch 3 sps and 1 sc in the sc's from the previous row. (270 sc) Row 7: ch 3, turn, *sk next st, DC in next st, DC in st that was skipped, repeat from* across (Making X's) (see video for visual instructions) Row 8: Ch 1, turn, working in both loops, Sc across (270 sc)

Row 9-21: Repeat rows 2-7

Row 22-25: SC in each st across.

Fasten off, Weave in all ends.

#21. Lightweight Disco Lamps Scarf

For men with fun personality, you can create this awesome color and pattern scarf for men. This scarf can be worn almost in all seasons .

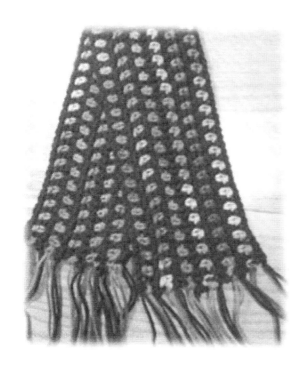

INSTRUCTIONS:

Front Single Crochet 81 in Black color and then Fasten off. Turn work. (WS)

Side 1

R 1- (RS) with Primary, join with single crochet to first front single crochet. *chain 1, skip next front single crochet, single crochet in next front single crochet, repeat from to last front single crochet.* Fasten off. And do not turn.

R 2- (RS) with Black, join with single crochet in first single crochet, single crochet in next chain-1 space. *Chain 1, skip next single crochet, single crochet in next chain-1 space, repeat from to last chain-1 space.* Single crochet in last single crochet. Chain 1, turn.

R 3-(WS) continuing with Black color, single crochet in first single crochet. *Chain 1, skip next single crochet, single crochet in next chain-1 space, repeat from* until 2 single crochet remain. Chain 1, skip next single crochet, single crochet in last single crochet. Fasten off. But do not turn.

R 4-(WS) with Primary, repeat R 2. Fasten off. But do not turn.

R 5-(WS) with Black, repeat R 3. Chain 1, turn.

R 6-(RS) continuing with Black, repeat R 2. Fasten off. But do not turn.

R 7-(RS) with Primary, repeat R 3 Fasten off. But bo not turn.

R 8-(RS) with Black, repeat R 2. Fasten off the yarn.

Side 2

Repeat Rs 1-8 working across the bottom edge of front single crochet Row.

Fringe

Prepare 14 pieces with each 11" long of Black Yarn

Prepare 12 pieces with each of 11" long of Primary Yarn

You can work with a lark's head knot to attach Black yarns to the ends of Black Rows and Primary yarns to ends of Primary Rows. Trim fringe evenly.

Scarf Ideas for Kids

#22. Gingerbread Kid Scarf

This cute gingerbread scarf will look adorable around your kids' neck. Their friends will simply love it and wish that their mom will make them one, too.

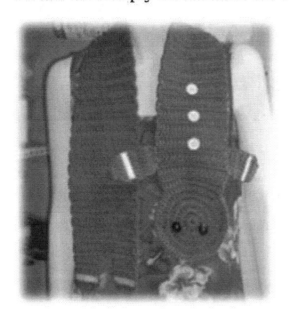

INSTRUCTIONS:

Rnd 1: Ch 3, 12 in 3rd ch from hook. Join with a sl st to 1st dc. (12 dc) Rnd 2: Ch 2, 2 dc in each dc around. Join as before. (24 dc) Rnd 3: Ch 2, 2 dc in same dc, dc in next dc. *2 dc in next dc, dc in next dc. Repeat from* around. Join as before.

Rnd 4: Ch 2, 2 dc in same dc, dc in next 2 dc. *2 dc in next dc, dc in next 2 dc. Repeat from* around. Join as before.

Rnd 5: Ch 2, 2 dc in same dc, dc in next 3 dc. *2 dc in next dc, dc in next 3 dc.*

Repeat from around. Join as before.

Row 6: Ch 3, dc in same dc. Dc in next 14 dc. 2 dc in next dc. Ch 3, turn. (18 dc) Rows 7 - 79: Dc in each dc across, dc in top of ch 3. Ch 3, turn.

For leg 1:

Row 80: Dc in next 7 dc. Ch 3, turn.

Rows 81 - 83: Dc in each dc across, dc in top of ch 3. Ch 3, turn.

Row 84: Dc in each dc across, dc in top of ch 3. Ch 2, turn.

Row 85: Dc in next dc (the ch 2 and this 1st dc count as a dc decrease). Dc in next 4 dc. Dc last 2 dc together. Ch 2, turn.

Row 86: Dc in next dc (the ch 2 and this 1st dc count as a dc decrease). Dc in next 2 dc. Dc last 2 dc together. End off.

For leg 2:

Row 80: Skip next 4 dc on Row 79 (right after the 1st leg), join with a sl st to next dc. Ch 3, dc in the next 7 dc. Ch 3, turn.

Rows 81 - 86: Repeat Rows 81 - 86 of 1st leg.

For Right Arm:

Row 1: Join with a sl st around the last dc of Row 11. Ch 3, 2 dc around the same dc. 2 dc around the last dc of Row 10. 3 dc around the last dc of Row 9. Ch 3, turn.

Rows 2 - 7: Repeat Rows 81 - 86 of 1st leg.

For left Arm

Row 1: Join with a sl st around the last dc of Row 9. Ch 3, 2 dc around the same dc. 2 dc around the last dc of Row 10. 3 dc around the last dc of Row 11. Ch 3, turn.

Rows 2 - 7: Repeat Rows 81 - 86 of 1st leg.

Add: black buttons for eyes, sew mouth with red yarn, sew white buttons as accessories (as seen in picture), sew and glue white picot ribbon on each arm and leg.

#23. General Kids' Scarf

Why I name it a General kids ' scarf? It is simple to make, functional, warm, and not easily dropped. My kids wear this one also.

INSTRUCTIONS:

Ch 72. Without twisting ch, sl st into beginning ch.

Round 1: Ch 1. Sc in the next ch and in each st around. (70) Round 2: *Sc in the next st, dc in the next st: Repeat from* to : around. (70) Round 3: *Dc in the next st, sc in the next st: Repeat from* to : around. (70) Round 4: Repeat Round 2

Round 5: Repeat Round 3

Round 6: Repeat Round 2

Round 7: Repeat Round 3

Round 8: Sc in each st around. Fasten off and weave ends. (70)

#24. Lego Pattern Scarf

Kids love lego, and they will be delighted to have a lego-themed accessories in their closet. This one is adorable.

INSTRUCTIONS:

Color 1:

ch 9

Row 1: sc into first chain from hook and across remaining 7 stitches, Row 2: ch 1, sc across,

Row 3: ch 1 sc first 2 stitches, pop stitch in the next stitch, sc in next 2 stitches, pop stitch, sc in last 2 stitches, Row 4-5: ch 1, sc across, turn **Color 2**

Row 6-7: ch 1, sc across,

Row 8: ch 1, sc in first 2 stitches, pop stitch in the next stitich, sc in the next 2 stitches, pop stitch in the next stitch, sc in last 2 stitches, Row 9-10: ch 1, sc across,

Row 11: ch 1, sc in first 2 stitches, pop stitch in the next stitich, sc in the next 2 stitches, pop stitch in the next stitch, sc in last 2 stitches, Row 12-13: ch 1, sc across,

Row 14: ch 1, sc in first 2 stitches, pop stitch in the next stitich, sc in the next 2 stitches, pop stitch in the next stitch, sc in last 2 stitches, Row 15-16: ch 1, sc across, turn **Color 3**

Row 17-18: ch1, sc across,

Row 19: ch 1, sc in first 2 stitches, pop stitch in the next stitich, sc in the next 2 stitches, pop stitch in the next stitch, sc in last 2 stitches, Row 20-21: ch 1, sc across,

Row 22: ch 1, sc in first 2 stitches, pop stitch in the next stitich, sc in the next 2 stitches, pop stitch in the next stitch, sc in last 2 stitches, Row 23-24: ch 1, sc across,

Color 4

Row 25-26: ch 1, sc across,

Row 27: ch 1, sc in first 2 stitches, pop stitch in the next stitich, sc in the next 2 stitches, pop stitch in the next stitch, sc in last 2 stitches, Row 28-29: ch 1, sc across,

Row 30: ch 1, sc in first 2 stitches, pop stitch in the next stitich, sc in the next 2 stitches, pop stitch in the next stitch, sc in last 2 stitches, Row 31-32: ch 1, sc across,

Row 33: ch 1, sc in first 2 stitches, pop stitch in the next stitich, sc in the next 2 stitches, pop stitch in the next stitch, sc in last 2 stitches, Row 34-35: ch 1, sc across,

Row 36: ch 1, sc in first 2 stitches, pop stitch in the next stitich, sc in the next 2 stitches, pop stitch in the next stitch, sc in last 2 stitches, Row 37: ch 1, sc across, turn Repeat rows 1-37 changing colors as desired until you read your desired length. Tie off and weave in any loose ends in.

Additional Accessories: For the ends, cut 4 pieces of each color yarn so they are about 6 inches long. Use one strand of each color and knot onto every other stitch at the end of the scarf.

#25. Ruffle Neck Scarf

Kid will love ruffle neck scarf because it looks pretty to pop up from their jacket or cardigans. They will feel as if they are Victorian princes.

INSTRUCTIONS

Chain 170.

Row 1: I tr in 4th chain from hook. I tr into each ch across. Turn.

Row 2: Ch 3. 1 tr into first tr. [2 tr into next tr, tr into next tr] repeat until end.

Rows 3 – 6: Repeat row 2.

Fasten off.

To finish

Join in yarn to first chain of foundation chain. Ch 1 and dc into each ch across.

Fasten off.

Conclusion

Thank you for downloading the book.

Upon completing the whole chapter of the book, you will learn a lot about 25 amazingly neat ideas for crochet projects of hats and scarves. Not only that, I also divide the book into several sub-headings so that you can easily locate the information you need.

In addition, I present the ideas based on the target audiences ' age and gender, so that you can easily choose the project you desire to make based on the purpose you have in making the project.

By targeting upper beginner level, I expect that I can help everyone who has just started their passion in crocheting to have it flourished and developed. This book is also suitable for you who wish to create something special for someone special to be given as a gift.

So, congratulation for purchasing this book! I hope that my writing will inspire you to improve your crocheting skills and executing them right away with collections of crochet ideas for hats and scarves.

Tunisian Crochet
20 Inspiring Crochet Patterns To Make Fashionable Crochet Projects

Introduction

Tunisian crochet is such a unique needle craft. It is actually not rare that those who are well-familiar with knitting and crochet have not discovered the beauty that Tunisian crochet can create.

Tunisian crochet is that kind of craft which combines the best of what crochet and knitting have to offer. Hooks used with this type of crochet look like normal crochet hooks, but the loops you make are kept on the hook all the time. Now, imagine all the patterns and effects you can make when you combine both the knitting and crochet techniques into one.

The fabric you create with Tunisian crochet is slightly less elastic and much denser than fabric created with normal crochet and knitting. Because of that, it is not really suitable for finer items like socks or baby wear, but this is the reason why Tunisian crochet is great for warm blankets and garments.

Actually, what this kind of crochet is famous for are afghans. These fabrics look like they have been woven rather than crocheted or knitted.

If you are not familiar with knitting and normal crochet, it will take you some time to get used to the way things work with this type of needle craft. If, on the other hand, you already know how to crochet or knit, learning how to make Tunisian stitches and patterns will be a breeze for you.

Once you learn the basic techniques used in Tunisian crochet, you can easily improve your skills and learn more stitches in order to achieve different pattern and color effects.

Also, if you are one of those who can't wait to see the finished item once they start a project, you will be more than happy to hear that with Tunisian crochet, it is faster to create fabric than with knitting and normal crochet.

As you will see once you take a look at the chapters to follow is that Tunisian crochet is not only easy to learn but also very satisfying to hook up.

Chapter 1 – Honeycomb Stitch Pattern

To practice this pattern, you can start with ten stitches of foundation row.

Row 1

You will begin your forward pass by doing *a Simple Stitch and then a Tunisian Stitch (move the yarn to the front, insert your hook side to side, yarn over and pull all the way through). Repeat from* all the way across the row till you come to the last stitch.

For the last stitch, I recommend that you stitch under the two bars there because of stability and to make a nice clean edge there. Simply yarn over and pull them through.

If you look at the stitches, all the Simple Stitches have a straight line whereas the Purl Stitches have a bump.

For the return pass, *chain one and pull through two loops. Repeat from* all the way across to the beginning of the row.

Row 2

For the forward pass of the second row, you need to alternate the stitches. So, here, you'll going to do *a Purl and then a Simple Stitch. Repeat from* all the way across until you get to the end of the row.

The return pass is the same as the previous one. Chain one, yarn over and pull through two. Continue in the same manner all the way across to the beginning of this row.

Row 3

The forward and return passes are the same as for the Row 1.

Row 4

Row 4, both the forward and return pass, is the same as the Row 2.

Continue alternating the rows until you get the desired length of this pattern.

Chapter 2 – Bar Stitch Pattern

Begin with a foundation chain of the desired length.

Row 1

Insert the hook into the first chain space from the hook, yarn over and pull up a loop. Repeat this all the way across the row.

Do the standard return.

Row 2

Find the horizontal threads over the spaces between each stitch. Skip the first stitch. *Insert the hook under the top horizontal thread, yarn over and pull up a loop. Repeat from* all the way across the row. Pull up a loop from the last.
The return pass is the same as for the previous row.

Row 3

Pull up a loop from the first space (alternating from the last row to keep the work even). Pull up a loop from each of the next horizontal threads to the last.
Skip the last space and pull up a loop from the last (alternating from the last row to keep the work even).

Do the same return pass as for the previous row.

Repeat from the second forward and return to make additional rows.

Chapter 3 – Basketweave Stitch Pattern

To start this pattern, you will have to work your basic forward and return row foundation.

Row 1

To begin the forward pass, skip the first bar and begin with the next one, the same as you would do with the simple stitch. Work three Knit Stitches, and then do four Purl Stitches. Repeat four Knit and four Purl Stitches all the way across the row. You'll actually do three Knit Stitches in the end because when you get to that final loop, you will do a Simple Stitch.

Your return pass is exactly the same as with the simple stitch. Yarn over and pull through one, yarn over and pull through two loops for the remainder of the row.

Row 2

Begin the forward pass by doing three Knit Stitches and four Purl Stitches. Finish the row in the same manner as the previous one.

The return pass is the same as with the return pass for the previous row.

Row 3 & 4

These two rows are the same as the first two rows.

Row 5-8

For the next four rows, you will make Purl Stitches where you've previously had Knit Stitches and Knit Stitches where you've previously had Purl Stitches.

The return pass for these rows is the same as with the previous rows.

Chapter 4 – Waffle Stitch Pattern

To begin, use a crochet hook to loosely crochet the basic chain because you will work through those back loops. After that, switch to your afghan hook and chain to your desired length.

For the forwards pass, skip the first stitch. *Go into the back loop of the next one, yarn over and pull though. Continue through the row going through that back loop repeating the same pattern from .*

To begin your return pass, yarn over and pull it through two loops. Repeat in the same manner until you come to the edge of the row.

Row 1

Now, you'll start with the first row going in the space between vertical bars. Go through that space, yarn over, and pull up a loop on your hook. Work in the same manner till the end of the row.

Go under those two chain stitches at the very end to start making a chain edge. Go up, yarn over and pull up a loop.

For the return pass, yarn over, pull through two and repeat this till the end of the row.

Row 2

To begin the forward pass, skip the first spot and move into the next space. Work in the same manner till the end of the forward pass. Go into the space between two vertical bars. Yarn over and pull up a loop.

To begin the return pass, yarn over, pull through two loops and repeat this till the end of the row.

Row 3

Row 3 is the same as Row 1.

Row 4

Row 4 is the same as Row 2.

Keep alternating these rows until you get the desired length.

Chapter 5 –Full Stitch Pattern

Begin with a chain of the desired length.

Row 1

To begin the forward pass, insert into the closest chain from the hook and pull up a loop. Continue pulling up a loop from each chain space, keeping all loops on the hook.

For the return pass, yarn over and pull back through one loop. *Yarn over and pull back through two loops. Repeat from* till the end of the row until you have one loop on your hook.

Row 2

To begin the forward pass, find the space between each set of vertical bars. Skip the first space and insert the hook into the next. Yarn over and pull up a loop. Work loosely to prevent curling. Insert your hook in the next space and pull up a loop. Continue pulling up a loop from each space in the row.

To go back, pull up a loop from the last space and from the last stitch. Yarn over and pull through one loop. *Yarn over and pull through two loops. Repeat from till the end of the row.*

Row 3

This row is the same as Row 1.

Row 4

Row 4 is the same as Row 2.

Keep alternating the rows until you get the desired length.

Chapter 6 – Spider Lace Pattern

For this pattern, you will need an odd number of loops. This example pattern is done with two colors. You will also need a double-ended hook.

Have a chain of the desired length and do a foundation row.

Row 1

Once you have loops of one color on your hook, slide the loops to the other end and turn the hook. Now, take another color. You can either make a slip knot and pull it through or simply pull through one and tie it off later.

To close the foundation row, begin closing through two loops all the way to the end.

Don't turn the hook now; you turn only when the hook is loaded.

Row 2

Yarn over, pull through two, and you now have three loops on the hook. *Yarn over, insert the hook under two bars and pull up a loop. Do that all the way across. Repeat from* all the way across.

Your hook is loaded now, so turn it.

For the return pass, begin with chaining one, then yarn over and pull three. Repeat this all the way across the row.

Row 3

In this row, you will work in the diagonal bars only. This is the yarn over from the previous row, and you will skip the other stitch.

Yarn over and pull up a loop. Because you are skipping that stitch, yarn over and pull up a loop in the diagonal. Repeat from all the way across the row. Don't yarn over for the last stitch.

The hook is loaded, so, turn it.

The return pass is the normal closing. Chain one, pull through one, *chain one and pull through two, repeating from* all the way across.

Row 4

Yarn over, go under two and pull through. Repeat this all the way across.

To close this row, chain one, pull through one, *chain one and pull through three loops. Repeat from* till the end of the row.

Chapter 7 – Drop Stitch Pattern

Start with a basic foundation row.

Row 1

To begin the forward pass, pull up a long loop. Now you'll do a Backward Purl Stitch (Tbps). Pull the yarn to the front, insert the hook into the space before the next stitch and grab the back vertical bar. Bring your hook to the front by going around the back vertical bar and between the vertical bars.

Pull the yarn back behind your hook, yarn over and pull up a loop. Repeat this stitch in each across.

For the return pass, yarn over and pull back through one loop, *yarn over and pull through two loops. Repeat the sequence from* all the way across. Hold the stitches while doing this to keep the tension even.

Row 2

Pull the yarn forward and insert your hook under the back thread of the next stitch pulling the yarn to back. Yarn over and pull up a loop. Repeat this stitch all the way across. Make sure that you are using the back vertical bar.

The return pass is the same as for the previous row.

Just repeat the two rows to make additional stitches.

Chapter 8 – Cluster Stitch Pattern

To begin, chain in multiples of four to the desired length plus two.

Row 1

Insert the hook into the first chain from the hook and pull up a loop. Pull a loop from each additional chain space keeping all the loops on your hook.

For the return pass, yarn over and pull through three loops. *Chain three, yarn over and pull through five loops. Repeat from* until you get to the last four loops. Yarn over and pull through the last four loops on the hook.

Row 2

Chain one, insert the hook into the closing chain of the first cluster, yarn over and pull up a loop. *Pull up a loop from each of the three chains in the first chain space. Pull up a loop from the closing chain of the next cluster. Repeat from* all the way across.

The return pass is the same as for the Row 1.

For additional rows, repeat from the second forward and return.

Chapter 9 – Lacy Simple Stitch Pattern

To begin, make a foundation chain.

Row 1

Insert the hook into the first chain space, yarn over and pull up a loop. Pull a loop from each additional chain space keeping all the loops on your hook.

To return, yarn over and pull back through one loop. *Yarn over and pull through two loops. Repeat from* all the way across.

Row 2

Chain one, skip the first vertical bar and insert your hook around the next vertical bar. Yarn over and pull up a loop. Work in the same manner all the way across the row. Pull up a loop from the last and chain one.

The return pass is the same as for the Row 1.

To make additional rows, alternate the rows 1 and 2.

Chapter 10 – Chunky Mesh Stitch Pattern

To begin the stitch, make a foundation chain in multiples of 2 plus 1.

Row 1

Work the basic forward and return row.

Row 2

With one loop on your hook, work *a Double Crochet (yarn over, insert the hook into the next stitch, yarn over and draw through, yarn over and draw through the first two loops on the hook).

Now, do a Purl Stitch (bring your yarn to the front, insert the hook into the next stitch pulling the yarn back behind the hook, yarn over and draw the loop through).

Repeat from * all the way across until the end of the row.

To return, do the basic return pass.

Row 3

Do a Purl Stitch into the next stitch. Then, do a Double Crochet into the next stitch. Repeat this sequence until the end of the row.

The return pass is the same as for the previous row.

Repeat rows 2 and 3 until you reach the desired length.

Chapter 11 – Crochet Coil Stitch Pattern

Begin with a chain of the desired length.

Row 1

Insert the hook into the first chain from the hook and pull up a loop. Pull up a loop from each additional chain space, keeping all the loops on your hook.

For the return pass, yarn over and pull back through one loop. *Yarn over and pull through two loops. Repeat the sequence from* all the way across the row.

Row 2

Grab the front vertical bar and pulling back slightly, move the hook under this thread from left to right while rotating your hook around so that it faces forward again. yarn over and pull up a loop. Repeat this across till the end of the row.

The return pass is the same as for the previous row.

To make additional rows, repeat from the second forward and return.

Chapter 12 – Tunisian Filet Pattern

Begin with a chain in multiples of three to the desired length plus four.

Row 1

Yarn over three times, skip four chain spaces, pull up a loop from the next, yarn over and pull through two loops.

Yarn over three times, skip two chain spaces, insert the hook into the next, yarn over and pull up a loop. Yarn over and pull through two loops. Repeat from all the way across the row.

For the return pass, yarn over and pull back through one loop, *yarn over and pull through two loops. Repeat from* all the way across.

Row 2

Chain two, *yarn over three times, insert the hook under the first thread, over the middle and then under the last thread, yarn over and pull up a loop (this pulls those two outer threads together to keep the spaces square). Yarn over and pull through two loops. Repeat from* all the way across.

The return pass is the same as for the previous row.

To make additional rows, repeat from the second forward and return.

Chapter 13 – Popcorn Stitch Pattern

Begin with a foundation row.

Row 1

To make a Popcorn Stitch, yarn over and *insert the hook as in a Simple Stitch, yarn over and pull through two loops. Repeat this two more times into the same stitch. Yarn over and pull through three loops.

Repeat from * wherever you want to apply a Popcorn Stitch.

To return, do the standard return pass.

You can make popcorns larger or smaller by inserting more or less into each stitch.

Chapter 14– Seed Stitch Pattern

Begin with a foundation chain in multiples of two. Do a foundation row in the same fashion that we would do for your Tunisian Simple Stitch.

Row 1

Begin the forward pass by skipping the first stitch. Do the Tunisian Simple Stitch (TSS) into the next stitch, *then do a Purl Stitch into the next stitch, and then a TSS into the next stitch. Repeat from* all the way across until the end of the row.

For the return pass, do the same as with the TSS; so, yarn over, draw through the first loop and then through two loops.

Row 2

Skip the first stitch, then do a Tunisian Purl Stitch into the next stitch, then do a TSS, a Purl Stitch, and then again TSS. Keep alternating the stitches until the end of this pass. When you come to the last stitch in the row, do a TSS.

The return pass is the same as with the previous row.

Repeat rows 1 and 2 until you reach your desired length.

Chapter 15 – Treble Stitch Pattern

Begin with a foundation chain of the desired length.

Row 1

Insert the hook into the first chain from the hook, yarn over and pull up a loop. Repeat till the end of the row.

The return pass is the standard one.

Row 2

Chain three, *yarn over twice, insert the hook into the next vertical bar. Yarn over and pull through two, yarn over and pull through two more. Repeat from* till the end of the row.

The return is the same as for the previous row.

To make additional rows, repeat from the second forward and return.

Chapter 16 – Pebble Stitch Pattern

Start with a chain in multiples of two and a basic or TSS foundation row.

Row 1

Insert around the first vertical bar as in a TSS, yarn over and pull up a loop. Pull up a loop from each additional bar across. Insert the hook through the last and pull up a loop.

For the return pass, yarn over, pull back through one loop, yarn over and pull through two. *Chain three, yarn over and pull through two loops twice. Repeat from* all the way across.

Row 2

Insert the hook in the first vertical bar from the hook and pull up a loop. Pull up a loop from each additional bar across skipping the chain spaces, pushing the chain spaces forward so that they come between the stitches you make now.

For the return, yarn over and pull back through one loop, yarn over and pull through two loops twice (alternating from the previous row). *Chain three, yarn over and pull through two loops twice. Repeat from* all the way across.

Repeat the two rows alternating in the return row to offset the pebbles.

The pebbles can be made smaller or larger by increasing / decreasing the number of chains in each chain space.

Chapter 17 – Raspberry Stitch Pattern

Begin with a chain in multiples of four plus one. Complete the foundation row.

Row 1

Pull the yarn forward, insert the hook under the front vertical bars of the next three together, pull the yarn back, yarn over and pull up one loop. (as in a Purl Stitch). This stitch is labelled as 3TpsTog.

Pull the yarn forward, Purl Stitch with the back vertical bar of the next, yarn over and pull up a loop. This is a Backward Purl. Then, do a Knit Stitch in the same and Purl Stitch with the front vertical bar of the same.

Repeat 3TpsTog in the next, then a Backwards Purl, Knit Stitch, and Purl in the next to the last.

The return pass is the standard one.

Row 2

Do a Backward Purl, Knit Stitch, and Purl Stitch in the next. Insert the hook in-between the vertical bars of the next three stitches from the back together, yarn over and pull up one loop as in a Trs. This is one 3TrsTog completed.

Repeat 3TrsTog in the next, do a Backward Purl, Knit Stitch, and Purl Stitch in the next, and work all the way across.

Do the standard return pass.

Row 3

Work in the same way as for Row 2 but alternate stitches from the last row – 3TrsTog in the next, Backward Purl, Knit Stitch, Purl Stitch in the next and all the way across. Pull up a loop from the last.

Do the standard return.

For additional rows, repeat from Row 2.

Chapter 18 – Reverse Stitch Pattern

With the reverse stitch, you use the vertical bar in the back so your hook stays behind your work. It's what makes it so difficult because you can't really see what you are doing.

Row 1

Skip the first vertical bar, push the hook through and grasp that back bar. It's a side-to-side motion. So, hook in the back, yarn over and pull through. Slip again the hook in three and go under that back bar, yarn over and pull up a loop.

Keep doing that till the end. Make your last stitch go behind two back bars, yarn over and pull through.

Do the standard return.

Chapter 19 – Crossed Tunisian Stitch Pattern

Create a foundation chain in multiple of 2 + 1. Do a foundation row.

Row 1

Skip the very first stitch and the next one. Work a Tunisian Simple Stitch (TSS) into the second vertical bar. Yarn over and draw a loop through. Make sure that you do this a little bit loose.

Then, bring your hook back to the first vertical bar and go through that stitch, then yarn over and draw through a loop. This is how you create your crossed stitch.

Repeat this across the row until you reach the last stitch in the row. When you come to the last stitch, you will do a TSS.

Complete the return pass as the standard one.

Repeat the forward and the return pass until you reach your desired length.

Chapter 20 – Ocean Stitch Pattern

To begin this stitch, you will need to create a foundation chain in multiples of ten plus two.

Row 1

Begin the forward pass by pulling up a loop into the second chain from our hook. So, insert the hook, yarn over and pull through. Pull up a loop into each chain all the way across.

For the return pass yarn over and draw through two loops, then yarn over and chain one. Yarn over and chain two, then yarn over and pull this loop through the four loops on our hook. This will create a chain of three and a shell.

Again, *chain two, pull through two, yarn over and pull through four loops. Repeat this sequence from* all the way across until you get to the last three loops on your hook.

When you reach these three loops, chain two, pull through one, yarn over and pull through all the three loops. This will make a half shell.

Row 2

Begin your forward pass by doing a chain one and then skip the half shell. Now, you'll start your repeat by inserting the hook into the next chain, *yarn over and draw through.

Then, pull a loop into the chain between the shells into the foundation chain. Insert the hook down into the foundation chain, yarn over and pull through. Make sure that all loops are even.

Skip the chain in the middle, go into the next chain and draw another loop through. Skip the next shell and that will end your repeat. Pull your hook into the first chain of those three chains, and repeat from * all the way across until you reach the last stitch in the row.

Pull up a loop in the top of the last shell.

For the return pass, pull a loop through the first one, chain one and start your repeat by *pulling a loop through four loops on your hook. Then chain two and that will end your repeat.

Continue from * and repeat all the way across until you reach the last five loops on the hook. Yarn over, draw through four, and chain one through the last two.

Row 3

Start your forward pass by chaining one. Then, skip the first vertical bar and pull up a loop in the next stitch chain. You will now start the repeat by *skipping the next shell and pull up a loop into the next chain.

Then, pull up a loop on the top of the shell in the row below. Go in the space there, yarn over and pull up a loop through. Pull up a loop in the next chain as well, and go into the third chain of the previous row.

Repeat from * all the way across. To finish the forward pass, skip the next shell and pull up a loop in the top of the shell in the row below. Pull up a loop in the top loop on the vertical bar.

For your return pass, yarn over and pull through the first two loops on the hook. Start a repeat by *chaining two, yarning over and pulling through four loops. Repeat from* all the way across. When you get to the last three loops, chain two, yarn over and pull through all three.

Row 4

Start your forward pass by chaining one. Skip the half shell, and start your repeat by *pulling up a loop into the next chain. Go into the shell below and pull a loop up there, and then do a loop in the third chain. T

hen skip the shell, and that will end your repeat. Repeat from * all the way across until you reach the last shell in the row. Now, pull up a loop in the top loop of the last shell, and this finishes the forward pass.

Do the return pass by yarning over and pulling through one loop on your hook. *Chain one, then yarn over and pull through four hooks on your loop. Finish the repeat by chaining two. Repeat from* until you reach the end of the row. When you reach the last five loops, chain two, yarn over and pull through four. Then chain one and pull through the last two.

Repeat rows three and four until you reach your desired length

To finish off this pattern, chain one, insert the hook into the vertical post and then draw that loop through the loop that is already on your hook. Do that into each vertical post all the way across.

Conclusion

Congratulations! You have learned 20 new Tunisian crochet patterns that will surely enrich your crochet projects. Although Tunisian stitches are widely-known for afghans, feel free to use the patterns that you have mastered with the help of this book for garments as well, such as cardigans, shawls, hats, scarves or sweaters.

All those lace patterns that you have learned to create are great for vests or cardigans, whereas you can use some denser ones for soft and warm sweaters to keep you warm on winter days. Hope you enjoyed this Tunisian crochet adventure and that you feel motivated enough to go grab your hook and yarn and show off your new skills.

Quick Crochet Projects:

Have Fun And Learn Amazing Crochet Patterns in 7 Days

Introduction

Since I know there are lots of you out there who think this kind of hobby is pretty cool, this book is not only for those who know how to read all those complicated crochet patterns but is also aimed to help all those who are eager to discover what the hook and yarn can do together.

When I got interested into crocheting, I really had some hard time with it. I couldn't understand all those abbreviations, didn't know what hook size to choose, how to decipher patterns, *etc.*

It appeared that all those great patterns that I found were only for crochet experts. So, amazing projects were simply out of my reach. Thus, I spent lots of time getting the hang of crocheting, and sometimes, this was really frustrating.

Because of that, I wanted to write a book with some simple yet great looking stuff that even beginners can make. So, I didn't want my book to have patterns with strange codes that most of couldn't understand. Instead, I wanted a book that will be beginner-friendly and that will spark readers' interest into crocheting.

Those who already familiar with single, double or triple crochet may also find the projects in this book inspiring. At first glance, all of these may look simple to make, but they are amazing as they give those more experienced ones a chance to make modifications and create their own unique patterns.

Beginners, I hope you will find crocheting as relaxing, inspiring and creative as I do. And all of you who already know how much rewarding crocheting can be, feel free to use this book as your source of inspiration. Happy crocheting!

Chapter 1 – Beginners, Get A Grip

When starting any kind of project, the first things you need are tools and materials. To make sure that you will pull off these projects successfully, a few things have to be explained here. This chapter, together with the one to follow, will be particularly useful for beginners.

Hooks

So, let's first take a look at the hook, a simple little tool that can do magic with yarn.

There are two types of hooks: steel hooks and yarn hooks. Yarn hooks are used with yarn, and they can be made of plastic, aluminum, bone, and hardwoods. I advise you to use an aluminum hook as they are great for beginners since they are not only inexpensive but are also available, durable, and easy to hold.

On the other hand, steel crochet hooks are used with some types of thread, such as linen and cotton. So, you may want to use these with some finer projects.

Hooks are available in different sizes. Beginners, for the time being, I recommend you use an H/8 hook made of aluminum. You will find it easy to make movements than with some large or finer hooks.

How to hold the hook?

Generally, there are two ways to hold the hook.

We call the first method the knife method. To hold the hook this way, place your right hand over the hook so that it rests between your index finger and thumb. You will control the yarn and hold the stitches with your left hand.

The second method is called the pencil method. You just hold the hook the same way you would hold a pencil, grasping it between your index finger and thumb.

Try out both methods to see which one is more comfortable to you. Lefties can reverse the instructions, or they can even learn to crochet this way.

Yarns

I love yarn shops because of this vast field of yarns that I can choose from. There are so many natural fibers you can use for your crochet projects, such as alpaca, cotton, cashmere, silk, and linen. And now think about all the colors that these gorgeous yarns can come into.

Yarns are generally classified by their weight, which actually refers to the thickness of the yarn. So, there you can find superfine to superbulky yarns, *i.e.* from the thinnest to the thickest.

For each weight yarn, there is a hook size you are supposed to use. Basically, the finer the yarn, the smaller the hook size. However, as with anything else, there are exceptions so that for some things like lace patterns, you will have to use a fine yarn.

With the hook I recommended you, you will need 4-ply knitting worsted weight yarn. When choosing the material, you may want to avoid cotton because it is not that elastic so that beginners may find it hard to crotchet with it.

As for the color, stay away from dark colors, at least during your practice phases, because the stitches will be harder to see.

When holding the yarn, you have to remember that two essential things here are to breathe and to relax. If you hold the yarn tightly, you will find it hard to work. At first, you may get frustrated, but you'll get used to it with a little practice.

To practice, hold the hook in your right hand, and make a slip knot (you can read how to do this in Chapter 2). The free end of the yarn should be hanging down. Hold the yarn coming from the ball in your left hand so that the yarn goes around your index finger. And finally, anchor the yarn with your pinky. Hold the free end hanging down with your middle finger and thumb.

When crocheting, remember that your wrists should work whereas your arms should stay comfortably so that wrists can do their job. While crocheting, everything should go smoothly, so let the yarn go easily under your pinky and over your index finger while making your stitches.

You now know the basics of the tools you need for your crochet projects. It's time to learn what to do with these.

Chapter 2 – Grab Your Hooks And Let's Practice

To get comfortable with holding the hook and controlling the yarn, beginners will need some time to get used to all this. So, here are some basic things to practice. As you move on to the projects, you will encounter some other stitches as well, but don't worry, you'll get detailed instructions for all the stitches, so you can complete the projects successfully.

Make a slip knot

Take a yarn and make a loop. Insert the hook through the loop.

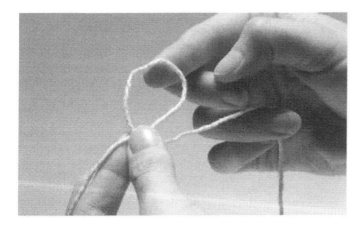

Pull both ends of the yarn so as to tighten the knot. Slide it up the hook and you are ready to move to making chains.

Make a chain stitch

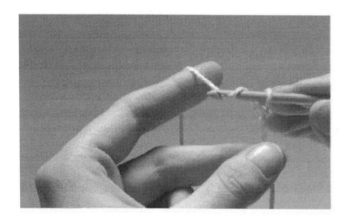

Hold the slip knot with your middle finger and thumb. The hook is in your other hand. Move the hook over the yarn to grab it. This is what we call yarn over.

Pull the hook, together with the yarn, through the loop. In this way, you will form your first chain stitch.

Keep doing this to get the number of chains you need (or as stated in a pattern). This is how a chain looks like.

Slip stitch or single crochet Insert the hook into your stitch and wrap the yarn around the hook. Pull through the loop and through the loop that was already on the hook. That is your slip stitch. If you want to continue making slip stitches, just insert the hook into the next chain so that you will basically keep repeating this step.

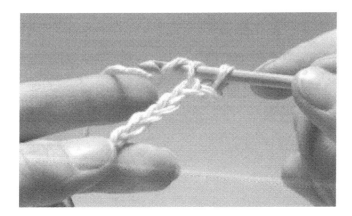

Double crochet

When double crocheting, skip the second chain and insert the hook under the top of the third. Wrap the yarn around the hook and pull through the chain loop. You will now have two loops on your hook.

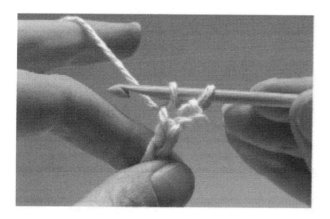

Yarn over and pull through both the loops. And there you have it, you made your first double crochet. You are now left with one loop on your hook so that you can go on working your next stitch.

When you finish one row of stitches, and you want to continue to the next row, turn your work and chain one. Since this is the turning chain, it counts as the first double crochet.

Skip the stitch which is at the base of the turning chain. Work one double crochet under the top 2 loops of each chain to the end.

Keep practicing until you start making stitches easily and smoothly. Then, you can try out these simple projects.

Chapter 3 – Crochet Leg Warmers

Get some time these winter days and crochet yourself a nice pair of leg warmers. The pattern is really simple so that even beginners will find it easy to make these cuties.

For this project, you will need the following:

- 2-3 skeins of the yarn of your choice (yarns that are of changing colors work great for this project)
- 6 mm crochet hook
- Scissors
- Darning needle

Step 1: Start by creating a slip knot.

Step 2: This pattern calls for 35 chains. You may make some modifications to fit around your leg. To make a chain, yarn over and pull through the loop. Continue until you get 35 chains. Make sure that this fits the widest portion of your calf. If you have to make more chains, you may need to buy another skein of yarn.

Step 3: Run your finger down the chain to make sure that it is not twisted.

Step 4: Fold it around to chain it with your first chain. Insert your hook into the first chain, take your working yarn, wrap it over your hook and pull the loop that you wrapped through both of the loops on your hook. You created a slip stitch. Now, you are ready to start on the first round.

Step 5: R1 — The entire pattern is worked using the double crochet stitch. To start this and any other round, first chain three. Locate the very next chain and double crochet the next chain there.

For you, beginners, this is how to work double crochet here.

Work into the very next chain. Yarn over and insert your hook into the back loop of the chain. Yarn over, pull up a loop; yarn over again, pull through the two loops, yarn over and pull through the remaining two loops.

Step 6: Work into the next stitch. For this round 1, pull one double crochet into every single chain. Make sure that you don't twist the chain as you go along. Go all the way across.

Step 7: You are now ready to complete round 1. Join your work with the third chain from your chain three, insert your hook into the chain, catch two loops and slip stitch. Yarn over and pull through the loop on the chain and on the hook. This is how you join or end each round.

Step 8: R2 – Make a chain of three and repeat the same process as for the first round. Again, at the end of this round, you should have 35 double crotches. When you reach the end of this round, join with a slip stitch, and start round 3.

Step 9: R3 – Begin in the same way, chain 3 and put one double crochet into every stitch.

Step 10: Repeat this until you get 28 rounds.

How to bind off?

To bind off, you can use a slip stitch. Cut the tail and pull it through the loop that was on your hook. Thread your darning needle, take the tail, and work it through several of the stitches, going back and forth to secure the tail in place.

When you get it woven in, cut the extra. Go to the other side of the leg warmer and do the same with the other tail.

Repeat the same steps to make another leg warmer.

Chapter 4 – Triangle Shawl

This is one traditional triangle shawl that will keep you warm on cold days. The pattern allows you to make it any size you need.

For this project, you will need the following:
- 3 skeins of the yarn of your choice
- 8mm crochet hook
- Scissors
- Darning needle

Step 1: Start by making a slip knot.

Step 2: Chain four and form a ring. To form this ring, insert the hook into the first chain, yarn over, and slip stitch that together.

Now, you can start your foundation for the triangle. In this pattern, you will have groups of four double crochets on the edges.

Step 3: Chain three and double crochet three more times. For beginners, this is how to do it. When you make a chain and yarn over, insert the hook into the center of the ring.

Yarn over and pull through as you do when double crocheting. Go ahead and do this 3 more times. All the time, you insert the hook through the center ring.

Step 4: Now, chain one to start off the next group. You'll always have to chain one to mark the groups.

Step 5: You can now go on double crocheting 4 times as with the previous group. That's the end of round 2. At this point, it will start to look like a triangle.

Step 6: Go on to start the row three. Chain three, turn your work like flipping a book page, and double crochet three more times.

Step 7: Chain one to give enough room to mark a group and to form a corner. Double crochet three times into the gap that you created with the first two rows. So, as you can see, this pattern consists of groups of 4 double crochets.

Work the following rows as the previous ones, flipping your work. Don't forget to chain one in between the groups of four.

You can work until you get the size you want. Some average size is 27 rounds.

How to finish off?

Leave a tail about 6 inches that you can weave in. Pull the tail through the loop that was on the hook. Thread a darning needle and find the densest portions of the pattern to weave in the end.

Chapter 5 – Crocheted Monsters

These little monsters are so cute that you should give this project a try and make your own monster collection.

For this project, you will need the following:

- Size E crochet hook, or your favorite one
- Small amount of worsted weight yarn
- Polyester fiberfill stuffing
- Plastic safety eyes
- White felt
- Embroidery floss

- Yarn needle
- Craft glue
- Embroidery needle

To make the head

Step 1: You will start from the top of your monster's head by making an adjustable ring. Insert the hook into the front of the ring, hook the yarn coming from the ball (working yarn), and pull up a loop through the ring.

Step 2: Now, you'll have to single crochet six rings. To do this, insert the hook into the front of the ring and pull up a loop of working yarn to the front. You will now get two loops on the hook.

Step 3: Wrap the working yarn around the hook from the back and pull through the two loops. This is one single crochet stitch. Do five more single crochets into the ring.

Step 4: When you pull the short yarn tail to close the ring, the stitches will come together to form a circle of stitches. This will make the base for your monster.

Step 5: By crocheting two times into each stitch, the circle will grow. Insert your hook under both loops of the next stitch as shown.

Step 6: As you pull up a loop, two loops will be on the hook. Wrap the working yarn around the hook and pull through the two loops. This is one single crochet stitch.

Step 7: To make an increase, single crochet into the same spot again. You will have to repeat this step for every stitch for this round, so you will get 12 stitches in the round. To count the stitches, look for and count V's around the circle.

Step 8: In the next round, you will have to increase in every other stitch. So, you will have to put two stitches in the first stitch, one stitch in the next, two in the next one, *etc.* There should be 18 stitches when you finish this round.

Step 9: In the next round, you will also do some increasing but in every third stitch. In this round, you should have 24 stitches. To do so, you will have to single crochet two times in the first stitch, and single crochet in the next two only once. Then, you should single crochet two times in the next stitch, and follow the same pattern until you come to the end of the round.

Step 10: Now, you should have a flat circle with 24 stitches around. When you single crochet around into each stitch for 9 rows, this circle will get a cylindrical shape.

So, to get this shape, use a stitch marker and crochet around your 24 stitches. Then, move the marker to the loop on the hook, and crochet around the 24 stitches again. Repeat doing this until you get 9 rows. If you want a shorter monster, you can do fewer than 9 rows. Similarly, if you want your monster to be a tall one, feel free to do more than 9 rows.

This is how the base of your monster should look like.

Step 11: To finish the base of your monster, you will have to cut the yarn leaving a few inches and insert your hook into the next stitch. Then, you should pull up a loop and pull it all the way through the loop that is on your hook.

Now, you will need the base.

To make the base, simply repeat the steps above to get a circle of 24 stitches.

Step 12: Before sewing these two parts together, attach the eyes. Cut a tiny slit in the center of these two circles or in the place where you want to insert the black eye.

Step 13: Decide on where you want to place the eyes, and push the post through each felt piece.

Step 14: To secure it, place the washer over the post inside the monster's body. Push to snap the washer onto the post and secure the eyes.

Step 15: Now, to give some shape to your monster, fill it with some stuffing.

Step 16: Fit the base part over the bottom of the monster's body.

Step 17: To stitch these two pieces together, use a yarn needle and the long yarn tail and sew the two parts.

Step 18: To give your monster some expression, you can use the embroidery floss and an embroidery needle to make some eyelashes, eyebrows, mouth, *etc.*

Step 19: If you want your monster to have teeth, you can cut a small piece of felt and glue it onto your monster's mouth. You can also glue the edges of the monster's eyes.

Chapter 6 – Crochet Roses

For this project, you will need:

- Crochet hook size 5.5mm
- Worsted weight yarn
- Darning needle
- Scissors

Step 1: Create a slip knot first.

Step 2: Make a chain of 60. Don't make the stitches tight because that will make your work a little bit inconsistent in the end, but you also don't want them to be really floppy. Create 3 additional chains.

Step 3: Now, you will have to double crochet. Beginners, listen up. Yarn over and insert the hook into the fourth chain from the hook. Insert into the first loop on top. Yarn over and pull up a loop.

Now, you have three loops on your hook. To complete the double crochet, you yarn over and pull through two and then yarn over and pull through the last two loops. It will look a bit stretched, but it will work itself out in the end.

Step 4: To finish this row, you want to add one double crochet to every single chain all the way across.

Step 5: For the next row, flip your work.

This is the last row that you will have to do, and you will have to create a scalloped edge here. This will create the petals of the flower.

Step 6: To create these scallops, yarn over and skip a stitch (don't count the one that is associated with your hook, skip the one next to it, and work into the one that follows). Basically, you will double crochet again. You will have to make 6 double crochets into each stitch.

Step 7: When you create a scallop, skip a stitch, and single crochet into the next one so that now you have two loops on the hook. Yarn over and pull through both. Now you have secured the scallop to your work.

Step 8: Continue this pattern all the way across.

Step 9: Cut your working yarn leaving the tail a bit longer. To bind off, wrap the hook around the tail and pull it all the way through the loop. Pull it tight.

Step 10: Your work already looks curly. You can start from the right side and roll the flower. Make sure that the edges match up at the bottom. Continue wrapping until you come to the end. You can pull the petals to get the shape you want.

Step 11: Thread a darning needle through the tail and flip the flower carefully upside down. First, secure the end of the flower, insert the needle, stitch it through some stitches on the other side and pull it.

Step 12: Now, start feeding the needle through all the layers so they don't fall through.

Step 13: Rotate the flower and do this again, back to the other side. Do this a few times. Now tie these two ends. If it is not sturdy enough, get another piece of yarn and feed it through the flower layers.

Chapter 7 – Puffy Fingerless Gloves

Make a pair of these puff fingerless gloves either for yourself or for someone else to keep you warm during winters.

For this project, you will need:

- 1 skein of the yarn of your choice
- 5mm crochet hook
- Darning needle
- Scissors

This will be done in two parts. You will first have to make the wrist part and then crochet the hand portion.

To make the wrist band

Step 1: Begin with the slip knot.

Step 2: Chain eleven.

Step 3: Skip the very first chain and single crochet into the second chain from the hook. Repeat that for every chain until you reach the end.

Step 4: When you finish this first row, chain one and flip your work. Make one single crochet into every stick but use only the back loop of the stitches. Each V in a row has a front loop (closer to you) and the back one. Work in the same fashion till the end of the row.

Step 5: To begin the next row, chain one again and flip over the work. You will have 30 rows worked in this manner.

Step 6: To join this together and form a band, fold it in half and make a slip stitch into every stitch. Work from the first stitch, grab the working yarn and pull through on your hook.

Step 7: Once you finish slip stitches, you can go on to bind off. Leave a little bit of a tail and pull it through the loop on the hook to finish it off.

Step 8: Weave in these two ends into the wristband using a darning needle.

To make the finger portion

Step 1: Grab a yarn and make a slip knot.

Step 2: Take the wrist band, find the line where it is joined, insert the hook in between a stitch, place the slip knot on the hook, and single crochet for every single row.

Step 3: Work all the way around the band.

Step 4: Once you reach the other side, join with a slip stitch.

Step 5: Count the stitches, and since you have 30 rows, you should have 30 single crochets.

Step 6: You will make puff stitches from round two to five. To begin a puff stitch, pull that working loop to be as tall as you want your puff stitches to be. Yarn over, insert the hook into that same stitch, yarn over, and pull up a loop.

Step 7: And again, you would pull up on that and again yarn over, insert the hook into the same stitch, yarn over, and pull up a loop. At this point, you have 5 loops on your hook, so work the same one more time.

Step 8: Once you have 7 loops on your hook, you are ready to finish off the puff stitch. So, you just have to yarn over, pull through all the seven loops, and you need to chain one to finish it off.

Step 9: Now, you are going to skip the next stitch and work the next puff stitch into the stitch over.

Step 10: Basically, you will repeat all this around.

Step 11: When you come to the end, you will join the puff stitches with a slip stitch. Grab top two loops from the puff stitch and slip stitch. Count the stitches; there should be 15 puff stitches.

Step 12: Do puff stitches to round 6.

Round 6 will have a thumb hole. When you make the right-hand fingerless glove, you'll start by making 12 puff stitches and then will create the thumb hole. For the left hand, create two puff stitches and then create the thumb hole.

Step 13: To make the thumb hole, chain 3, skip one place where you would normally have a puff stitch and you will add the next puff stitch to the place over.

Step 14: Continue along as you would normally would, putting one puff stitch into every chain spaces.

Step 15: Round 7 also consists of puff stitches. When you reach the spot where the thumb spot is, you will be decreasing slightly.

So normally, you will need to have two puff stitches, but here, you will put one into the thumb chain, so you will decrease a little.

Step 16: Join with a slip stitch.

Step 17: For round 8, make one puff stitch into every single stitch.

Step 18: Join with a slip stitch.

Step 19: Round 9 is the last one. This will be a single crochet border to this glove. Chain one and make a single crochet into every stitch.

Step 20: You will end up with 28 single crochet stitches. When you reach the other side, make your last single crochet into the last puff stitch, and make a slip stitch.

Step 21: Cut the yarn, bind off, and weave in your tails.

Made in United States
Troutdale, OR
07/16/2024

21261650R00201